D1275054

PRETTY POISON

PRETTY POISON
The Tuesday Weld Story

FLOYD CONNER

Barricade Books

NEW YORK

Published by Barricade Books Inc.
150 Fifth Avenue
New York, NY 10011

Printed in the United States of America.

Library of Congress Cataloging-in-Publication Data

Conner, Floyd, 1951–
    Pretty poison: the Tuesday Weld story / Floyd Conner.
      p.   cm.
    Includes bibliographical references.
    ISBN 1-56980-015-4 (cl)
    1. Weld, Tuesday, 1943–   . 2. Actors—United States—Biography.
I. Title.
PN2287.W4558C66 1995
791.43'028'092—dc20
[B]   95-22145
                                 CIP

Design by LaBreacht Design
First printing

C O N T E N T S

*T*uesday Weld was just the kind of girl Elvis Presley liked. He preferred kittenish girls, not more than eighteen years old, with shapely legs—all qualities Tuesday possessed. It seemed that their love was written in the stars. Tuesday asked her astrologer, Ben Gary, to prepare a horoscope. He said Tuesday was going to find her dream man: tall, dark, handsome, and extremely wealthy—a perfect description of Elvis Presley.

Getting past the incredible security which protected Elvis was a challenge—even for Tuesday. On her way to Elvis' penthouse at the Beverly Wilshire Hotel, she was stopped by security. She told them who she was, but they didn't believe that the casually dressed woman was a movie star. Tuesday was detained at the lobby for several minutes until one of Elvis' associates verified her identity and escorted her to his suite. By that time, Tuesday was in a rage. "Those fucking security people," she screamed. "I told them I was Tuesday Weld and those stupid bastards didn't believe me. Fuck! Fuck! Fuck! That pisses me off." Apparently Elvis was highly amused by her tirade. Another time, Tuesday dropped quart bottles of milk from the penthouse suite, just to watch them splatter on the sidewalk below.

Chapter 1

My Name Is Tuesday

The first question people usually ask Tuesday Weld is how she got her name. Over the years a number of stories have surfaced, many of them fabricated by Tuesday to amuse herself during the endless interviews she had to endure as a young star in Hollywood. She told one interviewer that she was named Tuesday because "two days" was the time her mother spent in labor. Another frequently circulated story was that she was born on a Tuesday. Actually, it was a Friday. One of Tuesday's most outlandish explanations was that she was named after the Goddess Tues. It was some time before anyone caught on to the fact that there was no such goddess.

On another occasion she remarked bitterly, "I changed my name to Tuesday because it was the day of the week the worst things happened to my mother."

Her mother, Aileen, tells a different story: "We had expected a boy and didn't have any girls' names ready. The hospital told us, 'Either you give the baby a name or she stays. That's the law.'" Mrs. Weld named the baby Susan because it was the first name that came into her head. "That was just so we could take her home," she explained. "We never called her that—and then suddenly it came like a flash. She looked exactly like a Tuesday. All people look like days and she looked like Tuesday."

The most plausible explanation was that her name resulted from a mispronunciation of her real name, Susan. As a small child she was unable to pronounce Susan, saying "Tu-Tu" instead. "Tu-Tu" eventually became Tuesday and the name stuck. Tuesday's version was that her mother had called her "Too-Too" because she was "too too everything."

Tuesday was sixteen before she had her name legally changed. It took her many years to accept her unusual name. When she was asked if Tuesday was her real name, she became so tired of answering the question that she would reply, "My real name is Benjamin."

"I used to think it was one of those crummy tricks my mother played on me," she said. "I like my name. I came in for a lot of jokes, but once I'm introduced, people don't forget it."

Susan Ker Weld, better known as Tuesday, was born in a Salvation Army hospital in New York City on August 27, 1943. Her father, Lathrop Motley Weld, was the black sheep of a wealthy, socially prominent New England family. Nicknamed "Babe," he was tall, with a handsome, lean face and penetrating eyes. A graduate of the Harvard class of 1920, he became a gentleman farmer on Cape Cod where he raised up to 3,000 chickens on his farm. Eventually, he gave up farming and moved to New York where he became an investment broker. He acquired the reputation of being a playboy and went through three marriages before meeting Tuesday's mother, Aileen.

Born in London, Aileen Weld had worked as an artist's model. She was the daughter of noted British illustrator Balfour Ker. An attractive woman with red hair, she became Babe's fourth wife. The marriage produced two other children: Sally (eight years older than Tuesday) and David (six years her senior).

Before Tuesday was born, her father developed a serious heart condition which prevented him from working. She was only three when her father died of a coronary at the age of 49. She was left with only one vivid memory of her father.

"I remember one thing about him. I remember one night it was raining and he came into the house dripping wet. Dad was tall—six feet four. He took off his hat and raincoat and squatted down and opened his arms for me

to come to him. I don't remember what he said. I just remember him squatting down and opening his arms to me."

Babe's untimely death left the Weld family destitute.
His heart condition had been so severe that no company
would insure him. Without a job or savings, Mrs. Weld
faced the prospect of raising three small children alone.
Her only hope was for financial assistance from her
wealthy in-laws. As Tuesday remembered, help was offered—on their terms.

"My father's family came from Tuxedo Park and they offered to take us kids and pay for our education, on the condition that Mama never see us again. Mama was an orphan
who had come here from London, but as far as my father's
family was concerned, she was strictly from the gutter. I
have to give Mama credit—she refused to give us up."

The family moved to a $20 a month cold water flat in
a tenement building on Manhattan's Lower East Side. The
apartment had a community toilet in the hall, although
there was a bathtub in the kitchen. To make ends meet
Mrs. Weld worked as a sales clerk at the department store
Lord and Taylor.

Tuesday became a child model almost by accident. Her
mother had a friend who was a buyer and designer at Best
& Co., another New York department store. She saw some
photographs of Tuesday from the family album and suggested that the beautiful child become a model. She
earned thirty-three dollars for her first modeling job for

a mail order catalog. Her mother gave Tuesday the first dollar she ever earned, her reward for remaining still for ten minutes in front of the camera. Tuesday used the dollar to buy a paper treasure ball containing little surprises.

For the next five years Tuesday worked as a fashion and catalog model for Best and Company. Mrs. Weld attempted to persuade her two other children to become models, but they refused.

Tuesday enjoyed being a model. "Modeling is such a glamorous world. What little girl wouldn't prefer it? You get out of school, and before I was five I knew how to put on pancake make-up and lipstick. I lived out a little girl's fantasy of being grown up."

Around the age of seven Tuesday lost her liking for modeling and resented her responsibility as the family breadwinner. "I became the supporter of the family, and I had to take my father's place in many ways...I was expected to make up for everything that had ever gone wrong in Mama's life. She became obsessed with me, pouring out all her pent-up love—her alleged love—on me, and it's been heavy on my shoulders ever since."

Her mother insists that she never tried to exploit her daughter. "From the beginning I knew that this little girl was creative," she said. She was determined to make sure Tuesday had every opportunity to find her niche.

Tuesday became one of the most sought-after child models in New York, largely because of her distinctive hairstyle. She was one of the first child models to wear a long, blonde page boy cut. At the time, the popular style for child models was tight, corkscrew curls.

As a result of the pressures of modeling, Tuesday began to withdraw into a shell. She became known as "The Rock" because she was stonefaced before the camera. "I didn't like photographers treating me like a piece of furniture," Tuesday recalled. "'Stand there. Move there. Sit down.' I got so that I became petulant and rarely smiled."

It became a challenge for photographers to devise ways to make Tuesday smile. "When I was eight years old, I was tall for my age," she remembers. "Almost as tall as I am now, which is five feet four and a half inches. It made me feel like a freak, and I was very shy anyway. Photographers had a terrible time getting me to smile. They tried everything; a jack-in-the-box, a mechanical bird that flew around the room. Nothing would make me smile unless I liked the photographers. They would jump around like monkeys. Usually I was happier when they gave me something to eat, either a great big lollipop or an ice cream sundae or some bubble gum."

Even as a child Tuesday was so shy that she often had difficulty communicating with others. "One of my biggest battles—or fears—is trying to relate and open up to someone," she admitted. "I'm very shy. People who are shy make my twice as shy. I don't know what to say. I clam up.

Gregarious people bring me out of myself. Yet I can't bring other people out of themselves."

She became withdrawn. "I was so painfully shy that I did not speak for years. I was modeling a slip for a mail order catalog and they wanted more flare in the skirt, so they cut it with a razor blade and slashed right through my leg, and I was so introverted I could not tell them I was in pain."

Despite her success as a child model, the Weld family remained poor. Tuesday explained that the outward appearances of success were misleading.

"I had pretty dresses and shiny patent leather shoes and a warm coat and a handbag and a pair of tiny white gloves. I had to look nice when mother took me on the rounds of agencies and advertisers, department stores and magazine offices. Everything I earned that was left over from our bare living expenses was spent on clothes. I was poor like the other kids, only I didn't look it."

Working as a model left her little time for play and other normal childhood pursuits. "I didn't have any friends when I was a child because I was haunting model agencies and posing for photographers when other kids were out rolling hoops—or whatever kids my age do."

Many of Tuesday's childhood memories were bitter. The other children in the neighborhood resented her pretty clothes and the attention she was getting. Some of the boys would push her and tear the black ribbon bows off her shiny Mary Jane shoes. They would taunt her and refuse to play with her. Without playmates, she retreated into her own imaginary world. Her favorite plaything was Jacob, an old, tattered beanbag which her grandmother had given her.

"I got attached to a little beanbag the shape of an egg, like Humpty Dumpty," she recalls. It had little crooked legs and arms attached to it. That was my little doll. All the other little girls in the neighborhood had dolls. Jacob had the most beautiful expression. The dolls all had the same expression, but I could change Jacob's looks any time I wanted just by twisting his legs or squeezing him. He was always interesting. He had an inquisitive look on his face all the time.

"The others always made fun of me and my beanbag. One day they grabbed him away from me and threw him into the gutter. They had a real laugh over that. I gave him a bath and he was fine the next day, but I cried for a week."

Not all her childhood memories were bad. One of her fondest memories was of a vacation to a Georgia farm with her brother and sister when she was five or six years old. Having spent her entire life in Manhattan, she was amazed by her first contact with nature. Everything she discovered evoked a sense of wonder.

"I discovered a chameleon. I discovered little red rocks in a brook and you could carve things out of the rocks and write with them. I discovered little chickens—it was the first time I ever saw one. Also a fox. I saw a baby calf born and a rattlesnake. I always had to have the first glass of milk which came from the cow that morning and it had all the original sour taste. I had to drink it because it was healthy."

The pressures of modeling, her strained relationship with her mother, and her lack of acceptance by the other children caused Tuesday to have her first nervous breakdown when she was only nine years old. She had become plump—partly because the photographers were always giving her candy and ice cream to make her smile. Her complexion had broken out in big red bumps which made her unhirable as a model. "When I was nine, I had a breakdown, which disappointed Mama a great deal. But I made a comeback when I was ten."

Unable to find modeling jobs for Tuesday, Mrs. Weld moved the family to Fort Lauderdale, Florida after she graduated from the third grade. One of the reasons for the move was that Tuesday's brother, David, was a promising swimmer and the best coaches were in Florida. Aileen Weld, a gourmet cook, tried running her own catering business. Tuesday felt even more out of place in Florida. "My mother moved me to Florida, but that didn't work. I felt like a citrus fruit. I just didn't fit in any where."

Mrs. Weld's catering venture failed, and she decided to take Tuesday back to New York to resume her modeling career. Tuesday had lost weight and her complexion had cleared up. Overnight, she had developed into a young woman. Although she was only ten-and-a-half, she could easily pass for fifteen.

Tuesday's mother recalled the reasons for returning to New York. "For two years Tuesday lived a natural life without a single day of posing of any kind. During this period I catered my favorite chili con carne to restaurants as far south as Miami. The children went to school; life was much more slow and peaceful. Then we started to run out of money and Tuesday became restless. I left the two older children with friends, and Tuesday and I went back to New York."

Tuesday resumed her modeling career in New York. By the age of twelve she had appeared on the cover of half a dozen magazines. She took drama and dance lessons and began appearing in television commercials. She studied voice with noted therapist Alfred Dixon. Tuesday played child roles on dozens of television programs including Playhouse 90, Alcoa Theatre, Kraft Theatre, and Climax. At first she had to completely memorize her lines because her sporadic education had left her unable to read properly.

"I couldn't even read. I'd attended seven different schools by then and never learned enough in any of them to read a complete sentence. I did my first bit part on TV when I was six. Mother had to read the lines to me and I would repeat them until I memorized them."

In 1955, the twelve year old guest-starred on *The Garry Moore Show*. She played a dual role as a teenager of the past and her modern counterpart. As the teenager of days gone by, she wore a dainty dress and a pony tail. Representing the teenager of today, Tuesday wore shorts and a man's shirt tied at the waist.

The pressures of auditioning and the constant fear of failure were more than the young girl could handle. She was only ten when she started to drink heavily. "I had my first cocktail at the age of five. I drank steadily for ten years. At the time it seamed a pleasure, not a problem…As a teenager, I was a wreck, I drank so much I can't remember anything. My teens passed by in a drink."

Tuesday insists that despite her denials, her mother was aware of her drinking problem. "Mother always felt if a fruit was forbidden, it would be wanted even more. She always let me drink, though." The child also consumed dozens of cups of coffee a day. A friend recalled that the ever present cup of coffee was Tuesday's security blanket.

Drinking alcohol was not the only vice Tuesday had picked up during her intense childhood. She became a heavy smoker, partly out of peer pressure. "I thought it was terribly chic," she said of her smoking habit. "I had an older girlfriend who smoked. So I'd just go around with her and try smoking, too. I made up my mind I was going to be the best smoker in town. I sat down one night, for three hours, and my girlfriend taught me how. She told me how to hold the cigarette, how to light it, how to flick the ashes—everything."

Cigarettes weren't the only things Tuesday was smoking. "I enjoyed getting high on anything," she admitted. "No, not anything. Not drugs like acid. The pot I smoked had to be a good quality, and I loved it. It gave you a terrific feeling."

Tuesday tried out for the lead in a Broadway play, *A Certain Smile*, but was rejected for the part because she was too young. She set her sights on becoming part of a little theatre group in New York which was made up of aspiring teenage actors. Although not yet a teenager, she passed herself off as sixteen so she would be accepted. "I began to wear heavy make-up, piled my hair on top of my head, put on high heels, and tight skirts. Kids my own age didn't seem to like me, so I tried to find acceptance in an older world...Being with grown-ups most of the time, I became one myself."

Even without the make-up and high heels, Tuesday could pass for a much older girl. Her once plump figure had developed into that of a shapely teenager. She had her first serious love affair when she was only eleven years old. She was twelve when she attempted suicide for the first time.

"I had fallen in love with a homosexual and when it didn't work out, I felt hurt...A bottle of aspirin, a bottle of sleeping pills, and a bottle of gin. I was sure that would do the trick, but Mama came in and found me. I was in a coma for a long time and I (temporarily) lost my hearing, my vision, and several other things. I decided that I should try to get some help, but Mama didn't think I needed analysis. She thought that it might look funny; after all, there was nothing wrong with her little girl. I ask you, who's the crazy one?"

Tuesday continued to have problems in school. Because she had missed so much school, her reading skills were far behind the other students. Tuesday claimed she did not learn to read until she was thirteen years old.

"I had been in and out of school so much, going on modeling assignments, that I hadn't been able to learn as much as the other kids my age. When I had to get up in front of the class to read, it was torture. I'd stumble over the simplest words, and everybody would laugh."

The experience was so painful that she skipped school whenever possible. "I was in and out of several schools, but I never really went. There were no rules in New York then protecting working children. I was doing television shows as well as modeling, and instead of going to school, I used to do what they called correspondence, which meant that I was working. I'd just write in and say I had jobs. Even when I didn't have jobs I'd get up in the morning and say, 'Goodbye, Mama, I'm going to school,' and then I'd head for the Village and get drunk. Sometimes I'd drink at bars, sometimes at parties, and sometimes I'd just stay home and drink...But then I wasn't a little girl at all at that age—I never had been."

Her older brother, David, was given the unenviable task of making sure Tuesday went to school. "My brother, David, was in charge of taking me every morning. We didn't get along. In fact, I couldn't stand him.... We had to take three buses.... I was awfully hard to get along with and David didn't help matters any. He used to tease me. I'd scream at the top of my lungs and throw my lunch money under the seats, which he had to retrieve. Or else, I'd wait until we got off the bus and toss my money in the street. I was such a sweet girl!"

In 1956, the Huntington Hartford Agency arranged for Tuesday to audition for the lead role in a low-budget teenage rock and roll film entitled *Rock, Rock, Rock*. It was one of the first films to capitalize on the rock and roll craze which was sweeping the nation. That same year Elvis Presley recorded his first number one hit, *Heartbreak Hotel*. Elvis was not yet known as the King of Rock and Roll. That title belonged to Alan Freed.

No one did more to promote rock and roll in its early years than Alan Freed. He was one of the first white disc jockeys to play the black music from which rock and roll was derived. Freed popularized the term "rock and roll" from a black slang expression synonymous with sexual intercourse. As a disc jockey in Cleveland and later in New York, Freed championed the new music. He staged the first major rock concerts and produced movies which featured rock and roll's biggest stars.

Freed signed some of the hottest performers in rock and roll to appear in *Rock, Rock, Rock*, including Chuck Berry and LaVern Baker, both of whom would later be inducted into the Rock and Roll Hall of Fame. Other headliners featured in the film were Frankie Lymon and the Teenagers, Johnny Burnette, the Flamingos, and the Moonglows.

The star attraction was Chuck Berry, one of the pioneers of rock and roll. As a youth, Berry had spent three years in reform school following a robbery conviction. Berry earned a degree in cosmetology and worked as a hairdresser prior to becoming a musician. In 1955, he recorded his first hit, "Maybelline," followed the next year by the hit "Roll Over Beethoven."

Tuesday Weld was selected over 300 other actresses for the role of Dori Graham. Once again, she lied about her age. "I was always lying about how old I was. When I made *Rock, Rock, Rock* in New York in 1956, I was only twelve— but I told everyone I was seventeen." Weld was paid $400 for her first starring role. The film, directed by Will Price (former husband of actress Maureen O'Hara), was filmed in only nine days on location in the Bronx.

Tuesday played Dori Graham, a teenager who wants to attend the school prom with her boyfriend, Tommy Rogers (Teddy Randazzo). Desperately in need of thirty dollars so she can buy an evening dress for the prom, Dori tries unsuccessfully to take out a loan from a bank. Informed that the bank is charging six percent interest, she decides to go into competition. She borrows fifteen dollars from her friend Arabella (Fran Manfred), which she plans to loan out at one percent interest. Not yet adept in the matters of high finance, she believes that one percent interest means she'll be paid back one dollar for every dollar she loans out. After a series of misunderstandings, Dori's father (Jack Collins) agrees to buy her the gown.

The musical highlights of the film included Frankie Lymon and the Teenagers singing "I'm Not a Juvenile Delinquent" and Chuck Berry's rendition of "You Can't Catch Me." Tuesday Weld's character sang two songs: "I Never Had a Sweetheart" and "Little Blue Wren." Since Tuesday was not a singer, a seventeen-year-old newcomer was hired to sing her songs. Her name was Connie Francis.

Once the producers discovered Tuesday's real age, they publicized her in their ads as "the New Sensational Thirteen Year Old, Tuesday Weld." Although the material was lightweight, the critics generally praised Tuesday's performance. She later admitted that the critical praise she received was an important motivational force early in her career.

"One thing that kept me going was the knowledge that so many people wanted to save me. Critics liked me, even though I was in horrible things like *Rock, Rock, Rock*."

Unhappily, many of the performers featured in *Rock, Rock, Rock* experienced personal tragedies which shortened their careers. In 1958, Alan Freed was charged with inciting a riot during a rock concert in Boston. The following year his career was destroyed as the result of his involvement in the payola scandal. Payola was a practice in which the record companies paid disc jockeys money under the table for playing and plugging their records. Despite being disgraced by the payola scandal, Alan Freed's contribution to rock and roll was so important that, years later, the Rock and Roll Hall of Fame was located in Cleveland, the city from which his broadcasts had originated.

Following the release of *Rock, Rock, Rock*, Chuck Berry recorded several top ten hits. His career was shattered in 1959 when he was charged with violating the Mann Act which forbids transporting a minor across state lines for immoral purposes. The charges were filed after Berry brought a fourteen-year-old girl from Mexico to work as a hat check girl in a St. Louis nightclub he owned. Although many believed that the charges were racially motivated, Berry was convicted and served two years in prison. Ten years later, Berry staged a comeback and recorded his first number one hit, the novelty song, "My Ding-A-Ling." Despite continuing problems with the law, including charges of tax evasion and marijuana possession, Chuck Berry was among the first inductees into the Rock and Roll Hall of Fame in 1986.

After singing Tuesday Weld's songs in *Rock, Rock, Rock*, Connie Francis decided to attempt a solo career. Her first nine records failed to make the charts and, in frustration, she was about to return to New York University when she was asked to appear on the first broadcast of American Bandstand. The song she performed, "Who's Sorry Now," became the first of 35 consecutive top 40 hits she recorded between 1958 and 1964. In 1974, Francis was raped at a motel following a performance at the Westbury Music Fair in New York. The attack left her emotionally devastated and she was unable to perform for years.

Even before she had appeared in *Rock, Rock, Rock*, Tuesday Weld fantasized about being a movie star. "I was good at games that required make believe. One of the favorite games of the girls was playing movie star. I'd be Mrs. Cary Grant and we'd pretend we had just come home from a fancy party. I'd make up dialogue as I went along and the others would follow me. It was wonderful while it lasted."

While Tuesday had starred in one movie, she was far from being a movie star. She continued to live in a run-down tenement building. She recalled a painful incident when she was thirteen. A young man wanted to take her to a high school dance. When he picked her up at home, it was immediately clear that he'd lost interest in her. "You'd think I was poison," she said.

To avoid further embarrassment, Tuesday made up stories about herself. She discovered that the more she lied about herself, the more she was accepted by her teenage friends. She told them she was born in England and frequently travelled through Europe. She claimed she had her own apartment and made clever excuses whenever anyone asked to see it. She told so many lies that she had to buy a notebook to record her stories so she wouldn't contradict them.

Tuesday sought religion as a comfort in her unsettled life, but she admits her conversion was brief. "When I was fourteen I was in dire need of something to believe in. So I went to look for God. It was four in the morning and it was raining and I was quite drunk. I climbed the steps of one church after another, but all the doors were locked. 'How can there be a God?' I asked myself. When they say, 'Oh yes, He's there but you can't go in if you're going to steal from Him.' Since then, I haven't believed in any God."

Tuesday continued to appear on television, acting in more than forty televised plays. In 1957, she appeared on NBC in the Goodyear TV Playhouse production of *Backwoods Cinderella*.

When she was fourteen Tuesday auditioned for the prestigious Actors' Studio. Its graduates included Marlon Brando, James Dean, and Marilyn Monroe. Once again, she tried to pass herself off as an eighteen year old, but when her real age was discovered, she was rejected. She was told, "There are certain things you just can't know when you're a little girl." Of course, they did not realize at the time that Tuesday Weld was not your average little girl.

That same year, director Elia Kazan announced he was holding open tryouts for William Inge's new play, *The Dark At the Top of the Stairs*. Tuesday claimed that she had fantasized about working with Kazan since she was ten. At the time, he was the most respected director in America. Born Ella Kazanjoglou in Istanbul, Turkey, he was the co-founder of Actors' Studio. On stage, he directed five Pulitzer Prize-winning plays including *The Skin of Our Teeth*, *A Streetcar Named Desire*, *Death of a Salesman*, and *Cat on a Hot Tin Roof*. As a film director his work includes *On The Waterfront* and *East of Eden*, films which propelled Marlon Brando and James Dean to superstardom.

Tuesday remembered being rejected for *A Certain Smile*, because she was too young. She was determined not to let it happen again.

"First of all, I bought the highest heels I could find," Tuesday recalled. "Then I found a bright, sleeveless dress that I knew Mr. Kazan couldn't help but notice, and to go underneath it, I bought a huge crinoline and taffeta petticoat that stuck out about a mile and made a swishing sound when I walked. I even dyed my hair platinum. Next came some deep-tan makeup so that I would look outdoorsy and healthy. To complete the picture, I bought some thick phony eyelashes that could have knocked people down if they stood a foot from me. I honestly felt that I appeared very sophisticated."

Elia Kazan did notice Tuesday and asked her to step forward.

"Young lady, how old are you?"

"I'm sixteen," Tuesday answered, even though she was only thirteen.

"Well can you tell me one good reason why you've made yourself up to look like a woman of thirty-five? Miss Weld, you're a mess! And another thing, that petticoat you're wearing, I could hear you coming a mile away."

Tuesday had to stand for what seemed like an eternity and endure Kazan's admonishment. She was shocked when he asked her to return the following week—minus the petticoat, false eyelashes, and deep-tan makeup. "Go home and scrub up, then come back as you really are and read for me again," he told her. She had to read several more times before she was selected as an understudy for the ingenue lead.

Tuesday earned less than one hundred dollars a week as an understudy. She turned down a chance to appear in a Broadway play starring Alfred Drake because she wanted the experience of working with Kazan.

"The understudies didn't belong," Tuesday recalled. "It was an awful, left out feeling…I was terribly lonely. I just sat alone in a place five flights up from the stage where the chorus girls would be if they had a chorus…It wouldn't have been so bad if you could read or something, but I and the boy who was an understudy had to run downstairs and be offstage voices during the play. We just chanted, 'Sonny Flood! His name is mud!' over and over again, teasing the child who was seen on stage. I'll hear it until I die."

In December, the lead actress became ill and Tuesday finally had her chance to perform on Broadway. Unfortunately, it was during Christmas week and the important agents were out of town for the holidays. When the actress recovered, Tuesday spent two more long months as an understudy.

Ironically, Tuesday was moping backstage, clutching a corsage of baby roses given to her by her mother to console her, when she was discovered. A man asked her what was wrong. He turned out to be Dick Clayton, the successful Hollywood agent who had helped to develop the careers of James Dean and Tab Hunter. He had come to the theater to congratulate his old friend, Elia Kazan, on his latest success.

Although she was wearing a plain black dress, Clayton was impressed by Tuesday's beauty. "It was a case of love at first sight," he recalled.

"You belong in Hollywood. You could be a star," Clayton told a stunned Tuesday.

"This girl had a special quality," he remembered. "I took one look at her, and I knew this kid had it—sex appeal, talent, depth."

Tuesday informed him that she was already represented by another agency. Disappointed, Clayton returned to California. Five months later, he was surprised to receive a telegram from Tuesday's mother. Her agent had been having difficulty finding Tuesday work and she wanted to know if Clayton was still interested in representing her. He replied that he would like them to come to California as soon as possible.

On April 18, 1958, Tuesday and her mother left New York for Hollywood. She was all of fourteen years old.

Chapter 2

Thalia Menninger

$\mathcal{D}$ick Clayton was at the airport to meet them. Since he had last seen her, Tuesday had gone on an eating binge and gained ten pounds.

"My gosh, Tuesday, you've grown into practically Wednesday!" he exclaimed. Tuesday quickly lost the weight.

There was no time for sightseeing. Clayton arranged for Tuesday to appear on *Matinee Theatre*, a local television program, that same day. He had shown photographs of Tuesday to Albert McCleery, the producer of the show. At first, McCleery was reluctant to employ an unknown actress, preferring one of Clayton's more established clients.

The agent persuaded him to take a chance on Tuesday and the episode, entitled "The Great Big Guy," provided an excellent role for her.

Tuesday and her mother moved into a tiny furnished apartment near the Sunset Strip. During their first months in California, the Welds moved several times.

"As I began to get work, we'd keep moving from one place to another until it seemed every time I finished unpacking, we were out looking for another apartment."

The first star Tuesday met in Hollywood was Tab Hunter. Born Arthur Geilen, he was given his distinctive stage name by his agent Henry Willson. Willson was the man who had changed Roy Scherer's name to Rock Hudson. At the time, Hunter was one of the most popular young stars in Hollywood and had recorded a hit song, "Young Love," which became number one for six weeks in 1957.

Hunter became friendly with Tuesday and escorted her to her first Hollywood premiere. At the premiere, she was interviewed and asked her age. Embarrassed to admit she was only fourteen, she said she was eighteen. Hunter told her that she should be proud that she had accomplished so much at an early age and to be truthful when she was interviewed. Although they rarely dated, Tab and Tuesday remained friends. When he received his own television show, Tuesday guest-starred in an episode entitled "The Doll In The Bathing Suit."

A few days after Tuesday arrived in Hollywood, her agent took her to the Twentieth Century Fox studio to meet Leo McCarey, who was producing and directing a new film entitled *Rally Round the Flag, Boys!* For more than thirty years, McCarey had been one of the top directors. In 1926, he had suggested the pairing of Stan Laurel and Oliver Hardy, who went on to become one of the greatest comedy teams in film history. In 1933, McCarey directed the Marx Brothers in, perhaps, their best film, *Duck Soup*, and four years later won an Academy Award for his direction of the classic screwball comedy, *The Awful Truth*. McCarey won a second Oscar for best director in 1944 for *Going My Way*.

McCarey was so taken with Tuesday that he cast her in the role of Comfort Goodpasture without even giving her a screen test. Dick Clayton recalled, "McCarey took one look at her and signed her right on the spot for the part of the sexy babysitter."

Rally Round the Flag, Boys! featured an all-star cast including Paul Newman, Joanne Woodward, and Joan Collins. Paul Newman was already one of Hollywood's biggest stars. In 1952, he was working as an understudy in the hit play, *Picnic*, on Broadway when he met a young actress from Georgia who was also an understudy. Her name was Joanne Woodward. Over the next few years, both Paul Newman and Joanne Woodward became major stars; she won an Academy Award for best actress in 1957 for her portrayal of a woman with a multiple personality in *The Three Faces of Eve*. In 1958, the same year they co-starred in *Rally Round the Flag, Boys!*, they were married.

The other rising star in the cast was a young English actress named Joan Collins. She had come to Hollywood after a disastrous first marriage to an English actor who had reportedly attempted to sell her to a wealthy Arab sheik for $10,000 in exchange for one night with her. Collins rejected this indecent proposal and divorced her husband. She became a star after playing the choice role of Evelyn Nesbit in *The Girl in the Red Velvet Swing* opposite Ray Milland.

Rally Round the Flag, Boys! is a comedy about suburban life in the 1950s. Henry Bannerman (Paul Newman) is an advertising man who lives with his family in historic Putnam's Landing on Long Island. He struggles to remain faithful to his wife, Grace (Joanne Woodward), a task made more difficult because his sexy neighbor, Angela (Joan Collins), is always trying to seduce him. The community of Putnam's Landing is thrown into turmoil when the military chooses it as the site for a top secret mission, which turns out to be the launching of a chimpanzee into space.

Tuesday Weld gave a scene-stealing performance as the Bannerman's teenage babysitter, Comfort Goodpasture. In one scene, she reads her own version of Cinderella to the children. "Cinderella's sisters were real cubes. Then that no-talent pumpkin turned into a T-Bird and Cinderella went to have herself a ball." After overhearing Tuesday's slang variation of the fairy tale, Newman asks his wife if the children were learning a foreign language.

In another scene, Tuesday welcomes a tall, young soldier who arrives at Putnam's Landing. When he speaks she squeals, "Ooh, a Southern accent. I go all ape." Objecting to her sudden infatuation is her boyfriend, played by Dwayne Hickman, who does a delicious parody of Marlon Brando in *The Wild One*. Unimpressed, Tuesday tells him, "Go away little man, flake off." A year later Weld and Hickman would again co-star in the television sitcom, *The Many Loves of Dobie Gillis*.

Tuesday made an immediate impression on Hickman. "Tuesday was only fifteen, yet, somehow she seemed more like thirty." Attracted, he asked her for a date. "Can't you see that you're too young for me?" she replied, disregarding the fact that he was nearly ten years older than she. "Besides, you act like a farmer."

Near the end of the film, the town stages a re-enactment of the Pilgrim's Landing. Tuesday is selected to play Pocahontas and livens up the pageant by performing a seductive Indian dance. The play turns into a disaster when the townspeople (playing the Indians) and the soldiers (portraying the Pilgrims) erupt into a free-for-all, as the Mayflower sinks in the harbor.

Veteran director Leo McCarey was another who was impressed by Tuesday's talent. "She's a bright young thing, quick to grasp, quick to absorb, and capable of self-discipline."

During shooting, Tuesday overheard cameraman Leon Shamroy remark that she looked like Jayne Mansfield's sister—from the rear. Tuesday vowed, "I can't wait until the day I look like a grown-up glamour queen from all directions."

Twentieth Century Fox insisted on signing Tuesday to a long-term contract, beginning at $350 per week. Her salary steadily increased and by the time she made *High Time* two years later, Tuesday was paid $25,000 with an option for a second picture at $50,000.

The publicity department at Twentieth Century Fox began a campaign to transform the not-yet fifteen-year-old Tuesday Weld into the next Marilyn Monroe. Many of Marilyn's old quotes were altered slightly and attributed to Tuesday. Monroe had said the only thing she wore when she slept was Chanel No. 5. The studio reported that Tuesday Weld sleeps only under a sheet of Eau de Cologne. It was well known that Marilyn Monroe did not wear underwear. Weld was quoted as saying, "I never wear underwear. It's much warmer with nothing on." Like Marilyn, Tuesday supposedly stood in front of a full-length mirror for hours, admiring her face and figure and applying make-up. The studio revealed that Tuesday's measurements were 36-19-35. "A slight exaggeration on both ends," Tuesday admitted.

One of Tuesday's most outrageous quips was, "I know it looks like I bite my fingernails. But it's not true. Actually, I have someone come in and bite them for me." In fact, Tuesday was a habitual nail-biter until she came up with a unique cure. "I was mad one night and I ripped them all off."

Suddenly, major publications were running feature stories about Tuesday Weld. *Newsweek* wrote: "In her day she has been called a lynx on the prowl, a combination of Shirley Temple and Jezebel, an enfant terrible." During the *Newsweek* interview, Tuesday lived up to the sex kitten image manufactured by the studio. The interviewer described Tuesday as she arrived, barefoot and dressed in a purple velvet bathrobe: "Her bottle-blond hair was a bramble bush, her eyes heavily mascaraed, her lips stroked with orange." With her legs crossed sexily, Tuesday blew smoke rings and said that she was looking forward to being able to pose for cheesecake photos. "I mean the real nude ones. I'm not old enough yet, though," she sighed.

The negative publicity did not hurt her popularity. Within a year of her arrival in Hollywood, Tuesday was receiving more fan mail and more attention in fan magazines than any other starlet.

Tuesday made no attempt to conceal the excesses of her personal life. She danced suggestively at parties and drank Lancers from the bottle. She downed Scotch-on-the-rocks with one gulp. She ignored the strict California liquor laws which forbade minors from drinking in public until age twenty one. At a nightclub she would order coffee, dump out its contents, and fill the cup with her date's champagne. Tuesday proclaimed her favorite sport was "shooting pool at a pool hall for special delinquents."

Once, on a dinner date, she arrived at the restaurant carrying a piece of cheese in the shape of an apple. She ordered a glass of milk and nibbled at the cheese without saying a word.

She defended her smoking habit. "I don't think it gives any insight at all into my personality...It doesn't say I'm smart and it doesn't say I'm stupid. It doesn't even say I'm nervous. All it says is that I smoke."

Tuesday was seen in public with dates her own age to men thirty years her senior. "I like all sorts of people," Tuesday said. "The ages of the fellows I date range from twenty-two to twenty-five, or even thirty-five. It doesn't bother me at all to date a man old enough to be my father. I like all types and all ages of men. I even like some ten-year-old boys."

An unexpected defender of Tuesday's dating habits was her mother. "Tuesday had already known quite a variety of boys. That's the way to do it. So many girls go steady with one boy for years, and then back off, and where are they? They haven't learned a thing." She added, "Of course, that can't be said about Tuesday."

Although she had not yet reached her fifteenth birthday, Tuesday had definite plans for her future. "First, I want to establish myself as an actress. On the personal side, my main aim is to learn more by reading, traveling, continuing to meet as many people as I can—and—for the time being, to stay single until I'm twenty-four. How can I make another person happy if I don't know how to live with myself? I want to learn to take care of myself completely."

"I am an enigma! I am the reincarnation of Lola Montez," Tuesday proclaimed. When asked if she was past the awkward age, Tuesday replied, "I went through my awkward age years ago, between nine and eleven." She proudly stated, "I don't pose as a model for anybody. If other teenagers are gullible enough to model their lives after me, that's their problem."

Years later, *Interview* magazine compared Tuesday's outlandish statements to those of Madonna: "But Weld encouraged misinterpretation: in a firework display of self-destruction she lit up the Hollywood celebrity press with acts and claims more audacious for their time than Madonna's are today."

Tuesday denied that she ever staged publicity stunts. "I never intentionally say anything to shock anyone. If I do, it's because I feel so strongly about a subject that I can't hold back. Moreover, I don't want to—or I'd become a suppressed human being. If I start worrying about what people might think because of what I say, whom I date, or how I dress, I'd be living in a constant state of concern.

Life is to short for that. If you feel like standing on your head, then, by all means, stand on your head."

She claimed that the media often distorted her actions. One evening a male friend suggested that they play pool. "I had never tried it, so naturally I loved the idea. It was my first time in a pool hall." The next day a local columnist wrote that Tuesday spent all of her time in pool halls.

Finally, Tuesday gave up trying to deny the stories. "Whatever they say is so, only more so. If I spent all my time trying to make people retract what they said, I wouldn't even have time to sleep."

Tuesday's already strained relationship with her mother reached the breaking point. Whenever Tuesday's mother interfered in her life, she warned her, "If you don't leave me alone, I'll quit being an actress—which means there ain't going to be no more money for you, Mama." Asked if she had any ill feelings toward her mother, Tuesday flashed a toothy smile and calmly said, "I hate Mama."

When Tuesday reached sixteen, she moved out and bought her own house. She explained that the main reason for the split was the built-up resentment she felt toward her mother. She reasoned, "If your mother sends you out to work as a model at the age of three, it is obviously why."

Tuesday's unconventional behavior outraged the Hollywood establishment which expected their young stars to be clean-cut and respectful. On occasion, Tuesday would mock traditional movie star behavior. She would make a movie queen entrance, holding a long, arched cigarette holder. Enveloped in smoke, she would say in a throaty voice, "I believe in glamour."

Louella Parsons, the aging gossip columnist and self-appointed spokesperson for the Hollywood establishment, was appalled. "Miss Weld is not a good representative for the motion picture industry. She called her "a disgrace to Hollywood."

After Parsons warned that she was a bad example for teenagers, Tuesday was perplexed about why she had become a target for the columnist. "I don't do a darn thing. I don't even read the papers. All these people go storming around about what I've said. I don't even know this columnist. All of a sudden she started on this hatred kick." Tuesday became so used to criticism that she was at a loss for words when something nice was said about her.

For Tuesday, all that mattered was that she maintained her faith in herself. "The only person I might be hurting is myself, and that's my own decision. Even if what I do doesn't seem to make sense, I'm not hurting anyone." She was willing to take responsibility for her lifestyle. "Actions speak louder than words—or money."

It seemed one of the few people in Hollywood who hadn't heard of Tuesday Weld was the distinguished actor, Sir Cedric Hardwicke. When asked his opinion of the controversial young star he replied, "What in heaven is a Tuesday Weld—some kind of weekday machine tool?"

Even more potentially dangerous to Tuesday's career was the perception that she was difficult to work with. She had the reputation of sometimes not knowing her lines. One director said, "Directing her is like pushing an elephant. She's very sluggish in reaching an emotion. Besides, she's a conceited, immature, irresponsible witch."

School continued to be a nightmare for Tuesday. "I went to public high school for a while. It was awful. Everyone treats you like a movie star—or looks at you surreptitiously and talks as you pass, or else they ignore you altogether. It didn't work out."

Tuesday hated school so much that she skipped whenever possible. "I never went to school on any regular basis, just slipped by—cheating. I never read anything but Nietzsche and stuff like that. So my whole frame of reference was mixed up."

Unlike New York, California had strict child labor laws. Tuesday was closely supervised by the Los Angeles Welfare Department. She was chaperoned on the set by an overzealous welfare worker whose job was to make sure she didn't smoke and to keep the men away. On the set, Tuesday was provided with a tutor and a tiny cardboard booth for privacy.

"Between the ages of fourteen and seventeen, I studied for ten minutes at a time in a cardboard box on studio sets…While they were setting up for the next shot, everyone else would be goofing off, but not little Tuesday. That was cram time with the books, and just when a cohesive thought might get together, the director would call for another take. They only way I kept from really coming apart was to pretend my schoolwork was another role I had to learn...Every studio had a different teacher in a different cardboard box. One week I had ten teachers."

Under these difficult conditions, Tuesday joked that she had learned to speak three languages: "English, pig Latin, and mumble talk."

Tuesday was more mature than her classmates and admitted she felt "old around teenage girls who giggle over boys." She was the center of attention at school when she appeared as Ricky Nelson's girlfriend on two episodes of *The Adventures of Ozzie and Harriet*. Ricky Nelson was the idol of millions of teenage girls, second in popularity only to Elvis Presley. Tuesday downplayed the experience of working with Ricky Nelson. "I like boys who talk," she recalled, and Ricky Nelson did not speak to her between takes.

Tuesday's brief experience at Hollywood High epitomized her education. Hollywood High was the most famous high school in America. Known as the "School of the Stars," its alumni included Joel McCrea, Mickey Rooney, Lana Turner, Judy Garland, Jason Robards, James Garner, Carol Burnett, Sally Kellerman, Stephanie Powers, and Linda Evans.

Tuesday Weld holds the distinction of having the short-
est tenure of any student in the history of Hollywood
High—less than one week. "I enrolled at Hollywood
High. It was a disaster. Nobody paid any attention to me
at all the first day I went to school. So the second day I got
all dressed in black—black dress, black hat, long black
gloves, black shoes. Oh boy, did I get attention. The principal told me to go home and change. I was causing a riot."

When a teacher told her that the black gloves were
creating a disturbance, Tuesday made up a story that she
wore them to cover a bad rash on her hands. She explained
that she suffered from a rare disease called Lacore, which
she had contracted in Mexico. The vice principal insisted
that Tuesday remove the gloves, but Tuesday refused. "I'm
a lady and ladies wear gloves," Tuesday informed him. "So
I'm going to wear gloves to school."

Every time she entered a class the teacher would ask
her name. When she told them, they would reply, "Yes, but
what's your real name?" One disbelieving algebra teacher
ordered Tuesday to write her name on the blackboard 100
times. Sometimes her mother would be called in to ver-
ify that Tuesday was her real name.

Tuesday occasionally missed class because she had acting jobs. One day a teacher at Hollywood High hassled her
for being absent. Fed up with being harassed Tuesday said,
"Listen, when I'm a big star you'll still be here making

peanuts." Thus ended Tuesday Weld's brief affiliation with Hollywood High.

Overall, Tuesday seemed to prefer California to New York. She was quoted as saying, "California is healthier for a girl than New York." She said that she preferred working as an actress to the "childish pleasures" experienced by most girls her age. "I don't miss not having an ordinary childhood because I've never known anything but this. I went to work as a model when I was barely four. I've been moving in a world of adults ever since."

Impressed by her performance in *Rally Round the Flag, Boys!*, Paramount asked Tuesday to audition for the part of Danny Kaye's crippled daughter in *The Five Pennies*. She came to the audition playing a Chinese flute, a ten cent present from her mother. "It helps me relax," she told director Melville Shavelson. It also helped her get noticed, and she was selected over seventy other actresses auditioning for the role. Shavelson recalled that once Tuesday got the part he never saw her with the flute again.

Tuesday welcomed the opportunity to work with Danny Kaye, who was considered to be the greatest all around talent in show business. The son of a Brooklyn tailor, Kaye made his dramatic debut as a watermelon seed in an elementary school play. As a teenager he worked the Borscht Belt as a clowning busboy and perfected his comedic craft touring the Orient.

The Five Pennies told the life story of bandleader Red Nichols. Nichols (Danny Kaye) arrives in New York to play cornet in Bob Crosby's Band. He falls in love with a show-girl named Bobbie (Barbara Bel Geddes) and forms his own band, The Five Pennies. Many of the big band greats, including Glenn Miller, Benny Goodman, Jimmy and Tommy Dorsey, Gene Krupa, and Artie Shaw, perform with Nichols.

The Nichols have a daughter named Dorothy. The young Dorothy (Susan Gordon) contracts polio while in a San Francisco boarding school. The doctors tell her parents that she'll never walk again. Red, guilt-ridden because he feels he has neglected his daughter, throws his prized cornet off the Golden Gate Bridge and gives up music. He takes a job in the Los Angeles shipyards to pay for Dorothy's medical bills.

Years pass and the teenage Dorothy (Tuesday Weld) celebrates her fourteenth birthday. Her friends at the birthday party don't believe that her father was once a famous bandleader. Red decides to attempt a comeback at a small lounge. Many of his old musician friends, including Louis Armstrong, welcome him back. Dorothy, who has been undergoing therapy, dances with her father.

The sweet, wistful Dorothy was a departure from the kind of parts Tuesday had been playing. Tuesday put on seven pounds of baby fat to look younger for the role. Melville Shavelson was impressed by her performance.

"Tuesday has a bright future," he predicted. "If she develops her natural talent and doesn't start relying on glamour, she'll be a fine actress one day."

Danny Kaye was amazed by Tuesday's preciousness. He quipped, "She's fifteen going on twenty-seven." He recognized her natural talent but sensed her personal life was in turmoil. "Tuesday was a dream to work with," Kaye remarked. "She seemed to have an instinct for how to act a scene. I also noticed she seemed to be heading for serious trouble...Stardom was well within her grasp, but she conducted herself in a manner that made you think she was just another Hollywood joke...it was as though she was some dizzy blonde with an empty head."

Danny Kaye insisted on doing all his scenes in one take because he believed he lost spontaneity with repeated takes. If he was forced to do a second take, he usually ad-libbed. This often caused the other actors to blow their lines.

Tuesday was asked to give numerous interviews to promote the picture. During a four day period, she was subjected to more than twenty interviews. She distrusted reporters and was uncomfortable discussing her life with total strangers. "I don't like interviews," she said. "It's impossible to sit down with someone and get to know them in a half hour."

In order to keep her sanity during the endless interviews, Tuesday fabricated stories about herself. Over the years, Tuesday had a hard time distinguishing between what she said and what was the creation of a publicist. "My quotes were probably the smart-alecky ones."

Sometimes she gave interviewers the silent treatment. On one occasion, a reporter spent an entire day shopping with Tuesday without her saying a word. It got to the point where it didn't really matter what she said. Nobody believed her when she told the truth, and often the truth was less believable than fiction.

Perhaps Tuesday's definitive role was Thalia Menninger, the golddigger girlfriend in the popular television sitcom, *The Many Loves of Dobie Gillis*. The show was created by Max Shulman, who had also written the novel on which the film *Rally Round the Flag, Boys!* was based. Shulman remembered Tuesday Weld and Dwayne Hickman from the film and gave them the lead roles of his new series. He was elated to have Tuesday Weld in the cast.

"A cliche, I know, but she really has star quality," Shulman said, "She pierces the screen. It's another case of a kid being a combination of a child and a woman."

The rest of the cast was also first rate. Dobie Gillis was played by Dwayne Hickman, who had appeared as Bob Cummings' nephew, Chuck, on the long running series, *Love That Bob*. Dobie's beatnik buddy, Maynard G. Krebs, was played by Bob Denver, who later went on to star in *Gilligan's Island*. Veteran character actor Frank Faylen was cast as Dobie's irascible father, Herbert T. Gillis. Probably the biggest casting coup was signing a little-known actor named Warren Beatty to play Dobie's nemesis, rich kid Milton Armitage.

Over the years, Warren Beatty has acquired the reputation of being Hollywood's ultimate ladies' man; however, his early years weren't so glamorous. He was so homely as a youth that he was nicknamed Henry because of his resemblance to the bald comic strip character. At the age of seventeen, Beatty got his first job in show business as a rat catcher for the National Theatre in Washington, D.C. During the performances, Beatty would stand in the alley behind the theatre and keep the rats out.

Beatty went to New York, where he earned his living as a dishwasher and a sandhog in the Lincoln Tunnel while living on a twenty-four dollar a month apartment. "I never intended to be a movie star," he said, reflecting on his career. One day he agreed to go to an audition to help a friend read for a part. His friend didn't get the role but Beatty did. For several months, Beatty appeared on a Sunday morning television drama, *Lamp Unto My Feet*, and played piano for an early morning religious program.

Tuesday Weld found doing a weekly television show to be a challenge. "What I'm doing now is the hardest thing I've ever done, routine-wise," Tuesday said. "There's no communication with the audience and everything is so fast. I'm a sort of teenage golddigger in it, and I think it's a wonderful part because it means something. I hate parts that don't mean anything. One must have growth, part-wise."

The pilot for the series, entitled "Caper at the Bijou," introduced Tuesday in the role of Thalia Menninger. Dobie meets Thalia, who quickly twists him around her little finger. She informs him that she doesn't date anyone unless he has money. In desperation, Dobie hatches a plot to rig a jackpot at a movie theater. At the last minute, he changes his mind and Maynard wins the jackpot.

Originally, Tuesday was signed for a single guest appearance. When the producer realized how good she was in the role, he decided to make Thalia a regular character.

The premise of the show was Dobie Gillis' desire to have just one "beautiful, soft, round, creamy girl" of his own. While he has several girlfriends, there is never any doubt that the "beautiful, soft, round, creamy girl" he wants most is Thalia Menninger. The only problem is that Thalia wants "oodles and oodles" of money and Dobie is not a very promising provider. She insists that she doesn't want the money for herself but needs it for her family. As Thalia reminds Dobie, "My father is sixty years old and has a kidney condition. My mother isn't getting any younger. My sister is married to a loafer and my brother will end up living off the county." Thalia is candid about her mercenary nature. "Even if my father had kidneys of steel, and if my mother was younger than springtime, or my sister was married to a jillionaire, or my brother was President of Harvard—I'd still want money!"

Most of the episodes featuring Tuesday Weld deal with Dobie's futile efforts to keep Thalia. The first episode, "Best Dressed Man," was one of the best. Thalia is so impressed by Milton Armitage's wardrobe that Dobie enlists the help of a clothing store owner in order to compete.

In the show's second episode, "Love Is a Science," Thalia tells Dobie it's time to stop wasting his time writing love poems and to start thinking about his future. She suggests that he study to become a doctor. She calculates that Dobie could charge ten dollars per house call and make one every ten minutes. They would be "rich, rich, rich!"

Another time, Dobie has to choose between Thalia and a rich girl named Whitney. Thalia only wants Dobie when he shows interest in the other girl and dumps him as soon as Whitney leaves town. On another occasion, the plot has Dobie cheating on a math test to get a good grade so he can show Thalia he has potential. Thalia soon brings him back to reality. "With all the money my father invested in these teeth, this face, this body, how can I use beautiful, expensive teeth to capture a pauper like you? The bait's worth more than the fish." She has a point.

Thalia Menninger became America's first teenage fantasy. In his *The Great TV Sitcom Book*, author Rick Metz wrote of Thalia: "She was stacked and so was her hair." Millions of American teenage boys had their first crush on Tuesday, which was fine with her. "I love it when somebody has a crush on me," she remarked.

The Many Loves of Dobie Gillis was the first television show to focus on teenagers and was one of the biggest hits of the 1959 season. As a publicity stunt, a feud was created between Dwayne Hickman and Tuesday Weld. It became apparent that there was really was a feud. Hickman preferred working with different actresses each week. "I can't get along with the same girl very long, especially actresses," he said. "They're a pain." According to Hickman, the biggest pain in the neck was Tuesday Weld. "She wasn't very professional," he remarked.

One of the barriers in the relationship was Tuesday's shyness. "Tuesday's not a very outgoing girl," Hickman observed. "She takes knowing. She doesn't give her friendship easily. On certain things she's outspoken, but basically she's reticent...Tuesday is always on guard. She doesn't trust anyone."

Dwayne Hickman expressed mixed feelings about his co-star. He realized that her beauty and talent were a ratings boost. "Beautiful, luscious Tuesday knew she had it all," Hickman acknowledged. "She was a naturally gifted actress." One of the reasons that she was so effective in the role was because in real life she shared many of Thalia's characteristics. "She was difficult, spoiled, petulant, and totally self-absorbed."

Tuesday was sometimes late or did not know her lines. One of Hickman's biggest objections to working with Tuesday was her reluctance to rehearse. He insisted on thoroughly rehearsing every scene while she preferred to go through each scene only once. Tuesday would mysteriously vanish between scenes, presumably to study for one of her classes. Exasperated by her unexplained absences, Hickman demanded that she run through her lines for a crucial scene. Tuesday refused, saying she needed to study for a biology test.

"Which is more important, biology or the show?" he asked her.

Without hesitation she answered, "Biology, of course."

The tension between Dwayne and Tuesday finally caused a heated argument in front of the cast and crew. Hickman told Tuesday that she was unprepared and unprofessional. It was his show and he didn't want it jeopardized by her behavior. She argued that it was her show just as much as it was his and she was just as concerned that it be good. A truce was called, but they never felt totally comfortable working with each other. "She was extremely immature and irresponsible," Hickman concluded. "I never really liked Tuesday." Apparently, the feeling was mutual.

"Tuesday was something else," recalls Bob Denver. He was amazed by the attention she received from the media. Between takes there was a media frenzy to get interviews. "The press was all over her. I'd never seen this brand of journalistic hysteria before."

For a while, she accommodated the reporters. Then one day she announced that she would no longer give interviews. At first, reporters didn't know how to react to her self-imposed silence. Tuesday openly expressed her disdain. "Beat the Press! That's the new TV show I'm doing."

In response, some reporters vowed never to print her name again. The press blacklisting slowed the momentum of her career.

"It was all too bad because Tuesday was on her way to stardom," Denver said.

Another distraction was Tuesday's insistence on bringing Wolf, her huge, ferocious white German shepherd, onto the set. As a child in New York, Tuesday wasn't allowed to have pets. She promised herself that as soon as she grew up she was going to buy the biggest dog she could find. Unfortunately, the dog sometimes disrupted filming and developed the nasty habit of biting director Rod Amateau.

Perhaps, Tuesday was really more suited to Maynard G. Krebs than to Dobie Gillis. She was nicknamed the "baby beatnik" and "The Queen of the Hollywood Beatniks" because she frequented coffeehouses.

"In Hollywood, I found they were the only places where people met in the evenings," Tuesday said. She fit into the bohemian atmosphere. She played the bongos and wore blue jeans, baggy sweaters, and often went barefoot.

"My idea of a good date is if I don't have to dress up," she said. "I'm complimented when I'm called a beatnik.

You identify the sloppy, unwashed characters who roam the Sunset Strip. People with no aim in life, no ambition, and, in most cases, no brains. These aren't beatniks, at least not as I understand the true interpretation of them."

Tuesday professed to be an expert on the subject, presenting an offbeat explanation of their origin. "The expression dates back to the fifteenth century, when it referred to intellectuals who fought for freedom of thought and expression. They were writers, poets, inventors, and painters. They were articulate, intelligent, and artistic. When someone calls me a beatnik, I accept it as a compliment—even if it isn't meant that way."

Eventually, she began to lampoon her image as a beatnik. When asked if she really frequented the coffeehouses, she replied, "I do once in a while. I have to keep the publicity going, you know. After all, they make it sound so interesting. I have to see what this is about." She acknowledged that her beatnik reputation resulted in a publicity bonanza. "If it hadn't been for that, I wouldn't have received half the publicity I've gotten."

She was perplexed why the way she dressed was considered beatnik. "If a black sweater, skirt, and long knit stockings are considered beatnik, then *Vogue* and *Harper's Bazaar* are beatnik magazines, because they have featured this type of fashion for years. I never have the time or patience to buy my own clothes. My mother always does it for me. If her taste is beatnik, so is Mamie Eisenhower's."

Tuesday ultimately denied she was a beatnik. "I don't really think there is any beat generation…I think the people who are beat are beat only because of the way they dress and because they go to coffeehouses and read poetry to music and beat bongo drums. I don't consider myself a beatnik, but very often, I go around in sneakers, jeans, and a dirty shirt. I think it's the neglected younger set. It's done to get attention."

Tuesday's nonconformity continued to get her in trouble. She was scheduled to appear on a television talk show. She had spent the day working on an episode of Dobie Gillis. Exhausted, she dozed off and didn't wake up until ten minutes before the talk show's air time. Frantically, she threw on a dress and put on a pair of high heels and raced to the studio. Getting out of the car she broke one of her heels. Not having enough time to go home and change shoes, she decided to go barefoot, assuming the cameraman would not show her feet. Instead, the interviewer concentrated on her bare feet, asking if it was done to get attention. Rather than explain what happened, Tuesday said, "I'm a beatnik."

The next day the papers carried a story that Tuesday Weld had appeared barefoot on the show, wearing what appeared to be a bathrobe. The incident heightened her image as a Hollywood rebel. Widely admired playwright and actor Sam Shepard wrote in his *Motel Chronicles*: "On an early TV talk show Tuesday Weld appeared in bare feet and a full shirt and the interviewer (I think it was David Susskind) spent the whole time putting her down for having bare feet on his show and how this was a strong indication of her neurotic immaturity and need for attention. I fell in love with Tuesday Weld on that show. I thought she was the Marlon Brando of women."

Dwayne Hickman found it increasingly difficult to work with Warren Beatty. Despite having only a minor role on the show, he already acted as if he were the huge star he would later become. Hickman remembers an incident when Beatty paused in front of a camera so he could comb his hair in the reflection of the lens.

Hickman recalls rehearsing a scene in an ice cream parlor with Beatty and Tuesday Weld. Beatty objected to the blocking because it emphasized his bad side. Once the scene was reblocked to his satisfaction, Tuesday complained that her bad side was being shown. By the time the scene was shot, Dwayne Hickman had his back to the camera.

Despite the popularity of Thalia Menninger's character, Tuesday's stint on Dobie Gillis would be short-lived. A few months after Dobie Gillis premiered on September 29, 1959, one of the program's sponsors insisted that Tuesday be dropped because the sixteen year old was too sexy for a family-oriented show.

Tuesday reacted by answering publicly that she would never do another television series. As a result, Tuesday evenings (the night the show was aired) were without

Tuesday Weld. Around the same time of Tuesday's departure, Warren Beatty also left the show. Director Elia Kazan, who had been indirectly responsible for the discovery of Tuesday Weld, cast Beatty opposite Natalie Wood in *Splendor in the Grass*, and the film made him a star.

Despite his personal differences with Tuesday, Dwayne Hickman conceded that she was an important part of the show. "I have always recognized Tuesday's talent as an actress and I believe she made an enormous contribution to the initial success of Dobie Gillis." Tuesday was so identified with the character of Thalia Menninger that there was never any thought of replacing her with another actress.

Director Rod Amateau had no doubts about Tuesday Weld's future in Hollywood. "She's a first-rate undisciplined actress with a God-given talent. But like any sixteen year old, she's full of fudge. She's misguided, not unguided. In another way, she's not sixteen, she's three thousand years old. She burns up the screen. Nothing is going to stop this girl short of a cataclysm—and I mean nothing!"

Chapter 3

I Was Lolita

In the fall of 1958, the number one best seller in the country was *Lolita*, a controversial novel written by Russian-born Vladimir Nabokov. The book told the story of a middle-aged man's obsession with a twelve-year-old girl. Although the book was brilliantly written, it had been rejected by at least twenty book publishers because of its taboo subject matter. The book went on to become so successful that the name Lolita became synonymous with a sexually precocious nymphet.

Almost immediately, Tuesday Weld was being called a real-life Lolita. She had earned the nickname "Tuesday Wild" because of her bohemian lifestyle. Journalists referred to her as the "archetypal nymphet" or "Shirley Temple with a leer." The roles she played in films contributed to her image as Hollywood's answer to Lolita. Tuesday described the characters she played as "little whore teenagers who would sleep with anybody but had a childlike quality."

The association was so strong that in September, 1959, *Coronet* magazine published a feature article on Tuesday in which she posed for a photo, holding a copy of *Lolita*. The article suggested that Tuesday Weld was the most exciting screen personality to emerge since Brigitte Bardot.

One reason for the Lolita comparison was Tuesday's preference for older men. Rumors circulated that she was dating men old enough to be her father, including Frank Sinatra and Raymond Burr. Her most publicized romance with an older man was with actor John Ireland. Best known for his Oscar-nominated performance in *All the King's Men*, Ireland was in his mid-forties when he met Tuesday. His seven-year marriage to actress Joanne Dru had ended in 1956. Tuesday tried to downplay her relationship with Ireland.

"John and I are only friends," she said. "We get along very well. We have a lot to talk about. It doesn't mean just because I've been seen at some party with John Ireland, or in some group with him, that we're having a romance." Aileen Weld explained Ireland's attraction to her daughter, "John likes children."

The fan magazines had a field day with the relationship. One article entitled "Make The Man Love Me" gave an account of Tuesday Weld's "hopeless love affair with John Ireland, a man three times her age." Tuesday defended her attraction to older men.

"People think that if I go out with a man in his forties, it is perfunctory that a lewd affair is going on. They can't understand that he would have a rapport with a girl of fifteen."

She saw nothing wrong with dating a man thirty years older, therefore she felt she had nothing to explain. "It's my life. I was born with it. I'm going to lead it. You have only one life, so live it."

Tuesday also preferred the company of older women to young girls. "I like to be with older women from whom I can learn something. There's no point in being with younger ones."

Since her father had died when she was three, it was suggested that her older boyfriends might be father surrogates. Tuesday indicated that it was more a matter of security.

"I'm sure it's because I like to be protected…There's more security with them. Older people just have more confidence in themselves. They have assurance. When you're around them it gives you a more confident feeling. That's why I open up more with older people than with younger people."

Tuesday recalled dating a boy her own age when she was fourteen. Although her date was very intelligent, she felt he was "immature socially." "He lacked assurance. I didn't feel secure with him. I couldn't relax. It was almost as if I didn't know whether I should pay or he should pay."

At one party Tuesday was surrounded by a group of Hollywood's handsomest young actors. Most young actresses would have been thrilled to be in that situation. She briefly listened to their mindless conversation before excusing herself to find a more stimulating discussion elsewhere.

Tuesday thought too much was being made of the age issue. "I don't think anyone should be limited to friendship based on age alone. It's putting a definite schedule on mental development." She insisted she was perfectly normal. "I have friends my own age, too. I'm not a freak!"

Her mother often disapproved of her dates. Whenever Tuesday insisted that her newest love was the one, her mother commented, "Sure, it's the real thing. It is every time."

It didn't matter to Tuesday if her companion was a jerk as long as his behavior was consistent. "If someone is really a bum, I have respect for him as long as he lives the role thoroughly."

The one turn-off for Tuesday was a man with a beard. "I've never dated anyone with a beard. If it was someone like George Bernard Shaw I would, though. He'd have to

Thirteen-year-old Tuesday Weld in her film debut in *Rock, Rock, Rock* (1958).

With Dwayne Hickman in *Rally Round the Flag, Boys!* (1958).

Danny Kaye, Tuesday Weld, and Barbara Bel Geddes in *The Five Pennies* (1959).

Reunited with Dwayne Hickman in the popular television sitcom, *The Many Loves of Dobie Gillis*.

uesday starred with Dick Clark and Michael Callan in *Because They're Young* (1960).

bian, Bing Crosby, Tuesday Weld, and Richard Beymer in *High Time* (1960).

Hand in hand with Paul Anka in *The Private Lives of Adam and Eve* (1961).

Lying in a hayloft with Fabian in *High Time* (1960).

In the arms of Elvis Presley in
Wild in the Country (1961).

Tuesday Weld, Elvis Presley, and Millie Perkins in *Wild in the Country* (1961).

Cheek to cheek with Jackie Gleason in *Soldier in the Rain* (1963).

Hiding in a closet in *Bachelor Flat* (1962).

The beautiful but deadly majorette Sue Ann Stepanek in *Pretty Poison* (1968).

With Ruth Gordon and Roddy McDowall in *Lord Love a Duck* (1966).

A Smiling Tuesday in *I Walk the Line* (1970).

be so fascinating I couldn't resist him. Then I'd overlook the beard. But generally, I think beards are dirty looking. Young fellows with beards...I've talked with a few of them. I didn't even hear them. I was so fixed on the beard, watching it move when the mouth moved."

Not every boyfriend was old enough to be her father. Her dates included Dennis Hopper, Tommy Sands, Tony Perkins, and Pat Wayne. One of her escorts was Edd "Kookie" Byrnes, one of the stars of *77 Sunset Strip*. Byrnes had the reputation of never dating the same girl twice, but he made an exception with Tuesday. She guest-starred on an episode of *77 Sunset Strip* entitled "Condor's Lair" in which she played Kitten Lang, a teenage novelist involved in a blackmail plot.

When director Stanley Kubrick began casting for the film version of *Lolita*, he wanted Tuesday Weld for the title role. The part of Lolita was considered the most sought after juvenile role in Hollywood history. Tuesday seemed to be the ideal choice but, as she would do so often in her career, she turned down a role which could have made her a superstar.

Mike Connolly, gossip columnist of the *Hollywood Reporter*, wrote: "Stan Kubrick's curiosity got the best of him...Stan sent for Tuesday...Too bad—Tuesday's too Monday's childish for Lolita."

Tuesday explained why she turned down the role. "I didn't have to play it. I am Lolita."

With Tuesday unavailable, Stanley Kubrick auditioned more than eight hundred actresses for the role before selecting an unknown, Sue Lyon. As expected, the role made her a star although personal problems ruined her career. Married at seventeen, divorced at eighteen, her second marriage was to a black football player. The prejudice she encountered because of the interracial marriage caused her to emigrate to Spain. Her third marriage was to a convict serving a forty-year prison sentence. The publicity surrounding the bizarre romance contributed to the decline of her acting career, which was finished by the time she was twenty-five.

Despite the tabloid stories, Tuesday's acting career continued to prosper. At the 1959 Golden Globe Awards ceremony, she shared the Most Promising Newcomer award with Angie Dickinson and Stella Stevens. That same year, she appeared at her first Academy Awards presentation. Along with Anna Maria Alberghetti, Connie Stevens, Nick Adams, Dean Jones, and James Darren, Tuesday performed in a production number accompanying the best song nominee, "Always in Your Arms" from the film, *Houseboat*.

Rarely was there a day that Tuesday's name wasn't in the news. It took a visit from a foreign head of state to upstage her. In September, 1959, Soviet Premier Nikita Khrushchev made headlines around the world by visiting California. A journalist wrote, "The Soviet Premier temporarily eclipsed Tuesday Weld."

As Tuesday's fame grew, she learned who her true friends were.

"It's like the night before you do a TV show, you've got one friend who will see you just to talk to you. Then the night after you do a TV show, you've got fifty friends you never knew you had. That makes you lonelier than ever."

Tuesday confessed that she suffered from loneliness. "I think that the main sadness that everyone has is loneliness. I think loneliness is the greatest torture a human can have. Rejection, insecurity, it all stems from loneliness. When I feel lonely, I suffer. I think or toss in bed. I don't call anyone."

Whenever Tuesday did use the telephone, her conversations were short and crisp. "Why waste time talking to someone on the phone for a half hour and saying nothing? It's gotten to the point when it takes about fifteen minutes just to say hello! The phone should be used only when you have something definite to say."

Tuesday began to test acquaintances, particularly boyfriends, to try to gauge their true feelings. "People seem to expect you to play games all the time. To me, that's living a lie. I used to play games," she admitted. "I'd think he'd like me better if I did this, if I didn't see him too often. What's the use of pretending you're something you're not? Selfishness is really what it is—because you don't want to get hurt, so you go back to the world of games. And it's not just playing games with boys—but with life—just playing games, deceiving for the sake of an impression."

She continued to be a favorite subject for the fan magazines. In 1959, *Screen Stars* magazine featured a story titled "Tuesday Weld and the Secrets of Her Past." Not many sixteen year olds could boast of having a past. She delighted in flaunting her anti-Hollywood lifestyle. When most stars wore expensive designer dresses, Tuesday wore short-shorts and sandals. "I don't see any sense in spending a thousand dollars for a dress to wear once," she said. This attitude made perfect sense—except in Hollywood.

Tuesday was so mature for her age that a rumor began circulating that she was a teenage impersonator. Even Tuesday had doubts she was really sixteen. "I'm beginning to think I'm much older than I am. I turned my ankle while dancing last week, and you know what they said to me? He took a X-ray of my feet and said my bones were not sixteen. The doctor said my bones were those of a nineteen-year-old girl. My feet are nineteen and my body is sixteen."

Tuesday burlesqued her image as a sex kitten. She posed for photos which parodied reigning sex symbols. One photograph showed Tuesday wrapped in a towel a la Brigitte Bardot. Another pose had her standing on steps, open mouthed and breathless, like Marilyn Monroe.

Tuesday enjoyed toying with reporters. She did some of her best acting during interviews. "I had the worst possible publicity. I decided to make up a whole life and say (to reporters), 'Come on, follow me,' and I'd do the most outrageous things I could think of. Part of it was true, and I couldn't tell you which—it was done in total rebellion because they were intruding on my privacy. Not because I wasn't outrageous, because I was. I'd just vamp. I'd do anything I could do to shock, and it became a part of me."

One person she didn't fool was her mother. "Tuesday makes up stories for newspaper reporters, because the truth bores her. She doesn't like telling the same thing over and over again."

Hedda Hopper, the legendary Hollywood gossip columnist, expressed grudging admiration when she wrote: "Tuesday was campaigning for recognition with no personal press agent and no studio publicity department writing for her. She did it with her own little hatchet—a sharp wit for one so young. And an eye and ear for the shocker. If going to a TV interview barefoot would make people write about her—she went barefoot."

Interviewer Mark Dayton was impressed by her intelligence. "Behind the innocent peaches-and-cream doll face is a remarkably perceptive mind that whizzes along at 100 miles per hour. There would seem to be four veritable facts about this sixteen-year-old individualist—that she is complex, that she is enchanting, that she is worthwhile, and that she is genuine." Actor Gary Lockwood, one of her boyfriends, attested to her verbal alacrity, "She's the fastest gun alive, she can deal with these taunts nicely or cunningly—whichever the situation demands."

Tuesday liked inventing her own words and was sometimes guilty of a malaprop. When she stopped eating meat for a time she declared, "I was on a vegetation diet." On another occasion, she described the inquisitive mind of ex-boyfriend Dennis Hopper by saying, "I think he's got a dilating brain."

In 1972, *Time* magazine suggested that many of Tuesday's conflicts as a teenager were caused because her lifestyle was ahead of its time: "Actually, Tuesday's sins—odd clothing, bare feet, and open love affairs would seem quite normal a decade later. Her chief offense was to be too hip, too soon."

The sex kitten image, which made Tuesday Weld too hot for television, was ideal for films. *Because They're Young* was Tuesday's first film in which she played a bad girl role. It was also her first portrayal of a teenage outcast, a role she would repeat frequently over the next few years.

Because They're Young starred Michael Callan, Doug McClure, and Dick Clark in his film debut. Clark had gained fame as the host of *American Bandstand*, a teen dance show which had originated in Philadelphia and later became a national hit. Like Alan Freed, Dick Clark had been called before the Congressional committee investigating the payola scandals. Clark was not indicted but he did divest himself of his financial interest in thirty-three businesses related to the record industry. The director of *Because They're Young* was Paul Wendkos. The previous year, Wendkos had directed *Gidget*, the teen hit which propelled Sandra Dee to stardom.

Tuesday Weld played the role of Anne, a student at Harrison High. Previously, she had an affair with Griffe (Michael Callan), a refugee from the switchblade set. She had broken off the relationship, but Griffe wants to renew it, claiming he has changed his ways.

Anne goes steady with Buddy (Warren Berlinger), the school's star quarterback. Buddy gets into a fight with Griffe over Anne and gives him a serious beating. The principal learns of the beating and threatens to suspend Buddy.

Anne reluctantly agrees to tell the principal the real cause for the fight even though her confession will ruin her reputation. When she arrives at the principal's office, she discovers that Griffe has already taken the blame, thus sparing Anne the humiliation of revealing her past.

Because They're Young featured musical numbers by James Darren and guitarist Duane Eddy. The title song, recorded by Eddy, reached number four on the pop charts. In those days, almost all teenage stars were encouraged by the studios to record albums, whether they could sing or not. Because of her popularity, Tuesday agreed to record an album, although she realized she was a much better actress than singer. The result was out-of-tune vocals accompanied by 1960's organ music. Lux Interior, a member of the rock group, the Cramps, and a collector of novelty albums, remarked after hearing the album, "How can Tuesday Weld be so pretty and sing so horribly?"

Tuesday Weld was becoming so popular that the studios were receiving huge volumes of fan mail addressed to her. Fan mail was one of the indicators the studios used to measure the popularity of their young stars. Not surprisingly, Tuesday was especially a favorite of young males, particularly servicemen. Tuesday Weld-related merchandise was marketed. One photo, current at the time, shows Tuesday, standing on a balcony and wearing a floppy hat, looking at a book of Tuesday Weld paper dolls.

Tuesday was still having trouble controlling her eating habits, which varied depending on her mood. At times, she would go on strict diets and hardly eat anything. Other times, she would go on eating binges, consuming as many as five thousand calories at a sitting. Tuesday described one of her culinary swings: "I was on a diet for a week! I ate nothing but hard boiled eggs, lettuce, and celery...But I've gone off. I really shot my bolt this week. I went to dinner last night, and started off with olives and Hershey bars, cheese, and a big pot of spaghetti, and three ice cream sundaes." Somehow, her eating binges never seemed to affect her appearance. As one observer noted, "None of it goes to fat. It all goes to beauty."

Tuesday celebrated her sixteenth birthday while filming *Because They're Young*. Tab Hunter visited her on the classroom set where she was presented with a cake by Dick Clark. For her sixteenth birthday, her mother gave Tuesday a Studebaker Lark convertible, the first of many cars she would own over the next few years. Tuesday specifically asked not to have a big party, explaining that receiving presents made her feel strange. Tuesday said, "On my birthday I'd like to go back to the old Chinese custom and give my mother a present."

Following her sixteenth birthday, Tuesday began assuming control of her life. She bought a $35,000 split-level home in the Hollywood Hills which she shared with her mother. She lived downstairs while her mother had an apartment upstairs with its own entrance and kitchen. One reason for the separate living quarters was Tuesday's resentment of her mother's interference in her love life. "How can I make a decision for myself, if I can't see someone?" she protested. Tuesday refused to let her mother on the set to watch her work. One studio associate observed, "When she's with her mother, you can't tell who's mothering who."

One of the reasons her mother objected to the separate living arrangements was because she couldn't supervise Tuesday's social life. "I don't know why Ma should worry," Tuesday explained. "She fears a girl my age could get in trouble with boys if she's living alone. If a girl is ready to get herself into trouble she can do it just as easily on a date while living with her parents and sixteen relatives!"

Tuesday began to show a more sensitive, reflective side of her personality. "I'm a big extrovert, which is only an introvert who has learned how to cover up her insecurity," she said.

She was on guard when she appeared in public. "There are always a lot of people around ready to help you get into trouble, but you have to get out of it yourself. So I don't go to parties much anymore. I like small groups."

"How small?" she was asked.

"Two people," she replied with a grin.

She especially avoided gossips. "When I go to a party where a lot of people sit around gossiping, I leave. Do you think the whispers about me will ever stop?" Tuesday insisted that many of the things printed about her were not true. "I'm just a young actress trying to make good. I don't know where they get some things."

Tuesday gave just enough interviews to satisfy the studio. She became more selective about whom she'd grant interviews. She was more comfortable with male reporters and said bluntly, "I don't want to talk with women." Eventually, she informed the studio she would only answer certain types of questions.

She experienced mercurial moods, ranging from exhilaration to despair. "If I'm terribly happy I just don't sleep at all, no matter how tired I am. Other times I'm terribly depressed. I remember once I stayed in bed for five days and the only time I got up was to eat. When I'm unhappy, I can sleep around the clock."

Tuesday rarely revealed her moods even to those closest to her. "I save my brooding. I cover it up. Then I'm twice as moody when I get alone. But when I get into those moods, I'm as much at odds with myself as I'm sure others must be with me."

When she became depressed or bored, Tuesday drifted off into the world of dreams. "All I want to do is sleep so I can go back into my dreams. I have fantastic dreams. Sleep is a great escape. I have dreams of escaping to the mountains—alone."

Not all her dreams were pleasant. She was haunted by a recurring nightmare in which she was blinded by thousands of lights pouring down on her. Between the lights, she could see strange faces peering at her.

More than anything else, she longed to be alone. "I like to be alone," she said. "I don't like being watched over. I don't like anybody hovering over me." Although she preferred solitude, Tuesday admitted she was lonely. "I'm always lonely. I like the warmth of people. Some people generate warmth. There are very few who actually do. I'm always seeking that kind of person."

Tuesday had trouble maintaining lasting friendships. "I always had difficulty keeping friends," she admitted. "After one month, I invariably lost interest in them. It's not that

I don't like people, it's just that I wish there were more people to like. When people give me a bad time, or talk behind my back, I can't really say I dislike them. You save your hate for something juicy. I'm just mainly indifferent about people who don't inspire or stimulate me."

Occasionally, she would lose her temper with people who did not live up to her expectations. "I get ornery, impatient, and snappy when I'm disappointed in people."

Tuesday liked to take long, solitary drives to get away from the pressures of Hollywood. "One of my favorite things is to be alone. Sometimes I like to be alone for a couple of days just thinking, writing, drawing, or driving up a new street that I never drove on."

Chapter 4

Sex Kitten

In 1960, Tuesday Weld starred in a college comedy for Twentieth Century Fox titled *High Time*. Based on a story by Garson Kanin, the working title of the film was *Daddy-O*. The movie was written originally for Spencer Tracy, but he became unavailable, and the role was rewritten for Bing Crosby.

Crosby was a show business legend, both as a singer and as an actor. Prior to Frank Sinatra and Elvis Presley, Crosby was the most popular singer in music history with sales of over four hundred million records. At the peak of his popularity, there was not a second any twenty-four hours when one of his songs wasn't being played on radio somewhere in the world.

High Time was directed by Blake Edwards. His step-father was a Hollywood production manager, and Blake spent much of his childhood on film sets. Edwards directed his first film, *Bring Your Smile Along*, when he was only twenty-three years old. *High Time* was his seventh film. His next project, the exquisite romantic comedy, *Breakfast at Tiffany's*, made him one of the most sought after directors in Hollywood.

The supporting cast of *High Time* included Richard Beymer, Fabian, Gavin MacLeod, and Yvonne Craig. The story concerns Harvey Howard (Bing Crosby), a wealthy fifty-one year old widower who decides it's high time he return to college to get his degree. He enrolls at Pinehurst University, where he is the oldest freshman in the school's history. His grown children think the idea of returning to school is absurd. Despite his age and wealth, Harvey asks to be treated like any other incoming freshman.

Harvey falls in love with an attractive French professor, Helene Gauthier (Nicole Maurey). Tuesday Weld plays Joy Elder, a husband-hunting student at the college. She expresses her interest in the much older Harvey. "It's just that I've outgrown younger men. I happen to find the mature male irresistible." By graduation, she is engaged to another student her age (Fabian). In the film's memorable finale, Harvey addresses the commencement audience and tells them, "I could no more get married than I could fly." Unexpectedly, with the aid of wires, he flies around the auditorium.

Crosby was known for his laid-back attitude on the set and he was frequently late. Finally, director Blake Edwards confronted him about his tardiness.

"Where the hell were you?"

"I was locked in a closet with twenty-four gypsies and a hot guitar," Bing replied. Edwards never asked his whereabouts again.

High Time was noteworthy for its innovative editing and unconventional storytelling. Blake Edwards experimented with an almost plotless storyline, which was not appreciated by some critics at the time. Bosley Crowther of *The New York Times* wrote: "But a few necessities are lacking. One of them is a script." Paul Beckley wrote in the *New York Herald Tribune*: "*High Time* has the distinction of being one of the few films with no story at all."

The score for the film was composed by Henry Mancini. Over the years, Mancini wrote some of his most memorable music for films Blake Edwards directed, including "Moon River," lyrics by Johnny Mercer, from *Breakfast at Tiffany's*; the title song for *The Days of Wine and Roses*, also with Mercer; and the *Pink Panther* theme. Actually, another song, "The Second Time Around," written by Jimmy Van Heusen and Sammy Cahn, overshadowed Mancini's compositions for *High Time* and was nominated for an Academy Award.

Tuesday made her own music during filming. Between takes, she and two other members of the cast, Richard Beymer and Jimmy Boyd, played an impromptu musical performance at the bandstand. Tuesday played the piano, accompanied by Boyd on the guitar and Beymer on the drums.

Tuesday, although a natural talent, continued to take acting lessons to improve her craft. She preferred playing comedy which, surprisingly, she found more demanding than dramatic parts. "It's more of a challenge than some serious roles," she observed.

The veteran Bing Crosby enjoyed working with Tuesday Weld. Asked about her future as an actress, Crosby replied, "Tuesday's got the right charms in the right places."

One thing Bing Crosby did not enjoy about making *High Time* was an actor's strike which stopped production for five weeks in March and April of 1960. The strike was called by Screen Actors' Guild President Ronald Reagan. Crosby was so angry with the delay that he called Reagan a "radical," probably the only time the future president of the United States was so described.

Tuesday Weld's name was being linked romantically with a number of young actors, including her costars in *High Time*, Richard Beymer and Fabian. One of her dates was so dazzled by Tuesday that he quipped, "When I'm with Tuesday, I just think the devil with Wednesday."

Tuesday's favorite date at the time was Richard Beymer. Beymer had come to California from Iowa at the age of ten. He earned ten dollars a week as a member of a kiddie group on a local Los Angeles television program. Beymer was fourteen when he made his film debut in *Indiscretions of an American Wife* starring Jennifer Jones. In 1959, he became a star with his performance in *The Diary of Anne Frank*.

They first started dating during the filming of *High Time*. One day the cast was at the airport, preparing to fly to Stockton, California. Beymer noticed that Tuesday was struggling with an extremely heavy suitcase. She was banging her legs black and blue with the luggage until Richard Beymer came to her rescue.

Tuesday was attracted to Beymer because of his assurance and maturity. He had a wide variety of interests: painting, sculpting, photography, and poetry. Tuesday discovered she could enjoy the company of a younger man as much as her older dates.

The fan magazines carried euphoric accounts of the young lovers. They speculated that Tuesday had found true love with the clean-cut actor. After a date with Beymer, Tuesday was quoted as saying, "I wish every day could be like this. I'm so happy." Beymer agreed, "I've never been in a romance as thick as this."

Mike Connolly of the *Hollywood Reporter* was more realistic when he wrote in April, 1960: "Tuesday Weld is in love with Richard Beymer. Or at least Tuesday was Saturday."

Richard Beymer explained the reasons for the breakup by telling an interviewer, "As much as I like Tuesday we discovered that we could find no promise of permanence in our relationship. She had things to do with her life and so did I. They were things which would have eventually sent us in different directions."

Tuesday was much more to the point. "We just didn't dig it together."

Never sure of his own acting ability, Beymer admitted he was intimidated by Tuesday and vowed never to work with her again. "That would be like working with a dog or baby," Beymer said. "Tuesday walks in and there isn't anybody else on the screen; she's too good, blots out all other performers."

The next year Richard Beymer reached the zenith of his career in the role of Tony in the film version of *West Side Story*. The film won ten Academy Awards, including Best Picture, but Beymer was still his own worst critic. "I climbed under my seat. I had to walk out of the theater. I just hated it. I looked like the biggest fruit that ever worked in film."

Tuesday had her own embarrassing experience at the opening of *West Side Story*. Her date was Timmy Evert, one of the stars of *Dark at the Top of the Stairs*. After the premiere, Evert escorted Tuesday to a party at the Ambassador Hotel. She frequently wore hairpieces, wigs, or false braids. That evening Tuesday wore a chignon, a coil of hair worn on the back of her head. On the dance floor they whirled faster and faster to the music. She could feel her hairpiece begin to loosen. Dizzy, she slid across the floor with her chignon flying in the opposite direction. Summoning up all the dignity she could muster, Tuesday said, "Excuse me, I think I lost my hair."

In 1960, Quigley Publications surveyed exhibitors to select the young actors who were most likely to achieve major stardom. Tuesday Weld headed the list, which included Jane Fonda, Angie Dickinson, George Hamilton, Stephen Boyd, John Gavin, Troy Donahue, James Darren, and Fabian.

Tuesday, still remembering her painful experience as an understudy on Broadway, had no interest in returning to the stage. She explained that the only way she would perform on Broadway was if she had "absolutely nothing else to do."

She discovered she became depressed each time she finished a film. "It's always very painful when it's over. Any movie. You get movie blues." When she wasn't working she was restless, eager to go on to the next project. "I have to keep my mind stimulated—thinking, doing things, reading. I go riding in the mornings, study dancing, singing. If you laze around when you're not working you go stale."

She became even more depressed when she didn't get a part she wanted. "I'd sit and wait and wonder what the producers thought of my screen test. My life seemed to center on that. Once I didn't get the part and I went into one of the greatest fits of depression and destruction. I drank a half gallon of vodka on the rocks...I ran around, screamed, and yelled and then took my car and crashed into things."

Her driving habits became notorious around Hollywood. She could be seen speeding through the night, barefoot and dressed only in a nightgown. Tuesday traded in cars as easily as the normal teenager changed clothes. "I can change my clothes as much as fifteen or twenty times a day. I had six cars last year. The one I liked the most was a Mercedes. After that I had a Lincoln Continental because I thought that was very elegant."

Like many child actors reaching adulthood, Tuesday began to have trouble getting good parts in films. "I looked too old to play young girls, and I wasn't old enough to play older girls."

Rather than continue to wait for a good role, Tuesday accepted a part in a low-budget comedy, *Sex Kittens Go to College*. The original title was *Sexpot Goes to College* (the film was later released under the title of *Beauty and the Robot* and *Beauty and the Brain*.) *Sex Kittens Go to College* was the inspiration of Albert Zugsmith, who had produced a series of teen exploitation films with titles such as *High School Confidential*, *The Beat Generation*, and *Girls Town*. The exception to Zugsmith's otherwise undistinguished career as a producer was *Touch of Evil*, a film noir classic brilliantly directed by Orson Welles.

Sex Kittens Go to College was Zugsmith's second film as a director. For the film he assembled one of the strangest casts ever featured in an American movie. Mamie Van Doren, the blonde bombshell who was a regular in Zugsmith productions, received top billing. Van Doren was the latest of a long line of would-be sex symbols who never succeeded in turning the public on. The rest of the diverse cast included *Route 66* star Martin Milner, comedian Louis Nye, former child star Jackie Coogan, veteran actor John Carradine, television horror show hostess Vampira, singer Conway Twitty, and the indescribable Woo Woo Grabowski. Zugsmith was fond of using relatives of famous stars in his productions. Featured in *Sex Kittens Go to College* was Mijanou Bardot, younger sister of the French sex goddess, Brigitte Bardot. Charles Chaplin, Jr. and Harold Lloyd, Jr., sons of legendary silent film comedians, also appeared in the film.

The science department at Collins College eagerly awaits the arrival of its new head, Dr. West. According to her resumé, the mysterious Dr. West has received degrees from thirteen universities and can speak eighteen languages. A large welcoming committee awaits Dr. West at the train depot. Jodie (Tuesday Weld) is a member of the band and plays a triangle as the train arrives. They are stunned to discover that Dr. West (Mamie Van Doren) is a statuesque blonde.

Jodie's main goal in life is to wear the fraternity pin of football star Woo Woo Grabowski. "I can't help loving Woo Woo," she confesses. She intentionally breaks a strap on her bra to trick the dim-witted Grabowski into giving her his fraternity pin to fasten the strap. Dr. West discusses the facts of life with Woo Woo and analyzes his fear of women. Jodie misinterprets the attention Dr. West is giving Woo Woo and tells her, "If you want him, you can have him. If Woo Woo wants a woman with built-in water wings then he's welcome to her."

The college learns that Dr. West is really Tassles Montclair, a stripper known as the Tallahassee Tassle Tosser. Jodie finally wins the affections of Woo Woo. She triumphantly sits in the back seat of his convertible and motions him, "Home, Woo Woo." Her true identity exposed, Dr. West agrees to leave the college.

During the filming of *Sex Kittens Go to College*, Mamie Van Doren became friendly with Tuesday. In her autobiography, *Playing the Field*, she wrote: "When I made *Sex Kittens Go to College*, in 1960, I met a young actress who reminded me of myself. Tuesday Weld was eight or nine years younger than I was but we immediately became friends. She was a wild youngster, always looking for excitement. Tuesday and I zoomed around Hollywood in the Vespa motor scooter I bought when I came home from Italy. We went to Palm Springs and spent a few days hitting the Racquet Club and other in spots of the Hollywood weekend crowd."

The film confirmed Tuesday's sex kitten image. Unlike most Hollywood sex kittens, Tuesday was a fine actress.

Film critic Rex Reed described her as "part sex kitten, part Duse." *Cosmopolitan* magazine dubbed her the "princess of pretend."

Against her better judgment, Tuesday agreed to star in another Albert Zugsmith production. The film, a fantasy, was entitled *The Private Lives of Adam and Eve*. Once again the movie was distinguished by Zugsmith's bizarre sense of casting. Mickey Rooney (who also co-directed the film with Zugsmith) played the Devil. Martin Milner and Mamie Van Doren, Tuesday's co-stars in *Sex Kittens Go to College*, portrayed Adam and Eve. Tuesday was featured in the role of Vangie Harper. Others in the cast were Fay Spain (as Lilith), Paul Anka, and Mel Torme. Zugsmith loved to introduce buxom blondes in his movies and his latest discovery was June Wilkinson (measurements 43-22-37). Hyped as Britain's answer to Jayne Mansfield, her American film career proved to be a "bust."

Actually, Jayne Mansfield was indirectly involved in *The Private Lives of Adam and Eve*. Zugsmith had wanted her husband, strongman Mickey Hargitay, to play Adam but Jayne was jealous of him starring opposite a rival sex symbol, Mamie Van Doren, and persuaded him not to accept the role.

The Private Lives of Adam and Eve marked a low point in the long career of Mickey Rooney. Born to show business parents, he made his first stage appearance at the age of one as Baby New Year. His mother suggested that he change his name to Mickey Looney (his real name was Joe Yule, Jr.) but he happily decided on Rooney. For three years beginning in 1939, Mickey Rooney was the number one box office star in America. As he grew too old to play juvenile roles, his popularity declined. Although he had earned more than twelve million dollars, he'd spent it all and he was broke. He filed for bankruptcy in 1962, partly as the result of the cost of six divorces. He could always count on finding work with Albert Zugsmith, who had previously cast him in *The Big Operator* and *Platinum High School*.

The practically nonexistent plot of *The Private Lives of Adam and Eve* concerns a stranded Nevada couple, Ad (Martin Milner) and Evie (Mamie Van Doren). In a fantasy sequence they are transported to the Garden of Eden where they become Adam and Eve. While in the Garden of Eden the couple must contend with the Devil (Mickey Rooney). The fantasy sequences were tinted in a process called Spectracolor.

During the filming, the already voluptuous Mamie Van Doren wore life-like rubber balloons over her breasts. Her long blonde hair was glued to the breasts to give her a Lady Godiva look. *The Private Lives of Adam and Eve* was condemned by the Catholic Legion of Decency as well as most film critics.

Tuesday kept "thought books," which recorded her observations on life. The books contained thoughts, short stories, and poems. "I don't do anything with them, just read them and keep them, maybe show one to a friend," she said. "I don't like to talk about them; it would be like reading the last couple of pages of a novel to someone who doesn't know what came before."

In her thought books she wrote comments about her films such as "I don't want to do it," or "I hate that part." However, she expressed no regrets about making the Zugsmith films. "I made the Zugsmith pictures because I wanted money and I wanted to work."

One of Tuesday's boyfriends at the time was another graduate of the Zugsmith films, John Drew Barrymore. He'd starred in *High School Confidential*, a Zugsmith production in which he dealt drugs to students from the glove compartment of his car. Barrymore had been born into the most distinguished acting family in America. His father was the legendary John Barrymore and his mother was the beautiful actress, Dolores Costello. He inherited his father's taste for fast living.

Handsome and virile, Barrymore married actress Cara Williams in 1952. One week after the wedding, he was jailed following a violent domestic argument. Over the years he was arrested on charges of drunken driving and involvement in a hit-and-run accident. Just prior to his divorce in 1958, the volatile and totally unpredictable Barrymore was arrested after what was described as a street brawl with Williams.

His relationship with Tuesday Weld was brief and stormy. Insanely jealous, Barrymore frequently argued with Tuesday in public. After they broke up, Barrymore continued to have brushes with the law and was arrested for possession of marijuana and other drug related offenses. He married actress Jaid Mako and their daughter, Drew Barrymore, became a popular child actress. Her personal life was also troubled; she admitted to an addiction to alcohol and cocaine before she reached the age of twelve.

On April 17, 1961, Tuesday attended the Academy Awards ceremony at the Santa Monica Civic Auditorium. Her escort was Sal Mineo, a nominee for Best Supporting Actor for his performance in *Exodus*. The son of a coffin maker, Mineo was so nervous that he had been unable to sleep for days. Unfortunately for Mineo, the Oscar went to Peter Ustinov for his performance in *Spartacus*.

Whenever possible, Tuesday attended school. Over the years, Tuesday claimed to have gone to forty-seven different schools (her mother placed the figure at six) as well as an endless succession of tutors. Because she was constantly changing schools and because of her celebrity status, Tuesday never felt she belonged. "Almost all my life, I've been an outsider," Tuesday said. "I was always standing on the edges of a crowd, so near I could reach out and touch them, yet never a part of them, because I didn't have their price of admission—conformity."

Her nonconformity was still reflected in her studies. While attending the Hollywood Professional School, she was required to take a psychology test designed to evaluate how a teenager would react to a variety of situations. The test was given in a multiple choice format. Tuesday, not being the average teenager, felt many of the questions had other possible answers. On those questions she didn't check any of the boxes and wrote in the margin: "None of the choices is very choice."

Tuesday graduated from the Hollywood Professional School in June, 1961. Despite her haphazard education, Tuesday had developed strong intellectual interests. She took piano lessons and continued to paint. She read books on art and began to paint in an abstract style. "My dabbling helps me appreciate more fully what goes into real art," she said.

Tuesday planned on going to college to study psychology, English, and music. Her musical interests ranged from folksinger Jimmie Rodgers to Russian classical composer and pianist Sergei Rachmaninoff. She read on a wide variety of subjects; her favorite authors were Sigmund Freud, Ernest Hemingway, and Paul Gallico. "I like Freud because he stimulates the mind," she observed. It turned out that her acting career kept her too busy to attend college.

TV Guide carried a feature on her entitled "Tuesday Weld—Girl Philosopher." Tuesday summed up her philosophy of life by saying, "When you're given a gift—

life—you shouldn't sit around waiting for a reason to open it." The article concluded: "As she enters teenage from the wrong side, Tuesday Weld is having a ball."

At seventeen, Tuesday Weld was already reflecting on her life. She described herself as being "young with an old soul." Tuesday said, "It's better being older. At least I got a lot of that behind me."

Her eighteenth birthday was an important milestone. Already she could see her life had passed through various stages. "I'll be eighteen in August (1961). Then I'll be free to work harder. Life falls in three cycles. First you're a child. You're free. You can do anything you feel like. Nothing stops you. Then you go through the second stage. I must have been around twelve years old when I reached the second stage—when people say you can't do this or you mustn't do that, and you find yourself hurt by things you do. Laws prevent you from doing things. You want to protect yourself, so you restrict the things you say and do. Then the third phase begins where you decide to untie the knots and be honest again. You're able to feel free again and express yourself, and what's inside you. That's where I am now."

When asked about her future, Tuesday replied, "I don't know the future. All I can say is that in five years I want to be up. That's all I can tell you. There isn't much point to talking about the past. I don't think very much about it except when something specific happens. And there's the present—that's now. I'm enjoying myself."

Chapter 5

Tuesday and Elvis

*I*n May, 1960, Tuesday Weld met Elvis Presley, who had just been released from the Army. They met by accident when they bumped into each other on the Twentieth Century Fox lot. Another account had them meeting for the first time after Tuesday telephoned Elvis at his suite at the Beverly Wilshire Hotel. Whatever the circumstances of their first meeting, it was clear that Tuesday and Elvis were instantly attracted to each other.

Elvis Presley was the undisputed King of Rock and Roll. During his career he sold hundreds of millions of records and had eighteen number one hits. This was a far cry from August, 1953, when he earned thirty-five dollars a week as a truck driver for the Crown Electric Company. From this salary he paid four dollars to record two songs at the Memphis Recording Studio. The session led to a recording contract with Sun Records.

Elvis was not an overnight sensation. At his first public appearance in Memphis, he received third billing (topping the bill was yodeling country singer Slim Whitman) and his name was misspelled. Elvis and his band, the Blue Moon Boys, toured the South accepting ten dollar a night bookings in high school gyms and roadhouses.

Gradually, Elvis Presley attracted a large following, particularly among females. His appearance at the Gator Bowl in Jacksonville, Florida on May 13, 1955, resulted in a near riot. Dressed in a pink suit and see-through shirt, Elvis worked the crowd into a frenzy. At the end of the set he joked, "Girls, I'll see you backstage." Hundreds of teenage girls chased Elvis backstage where they cornered him in his dressing room and began tearing off his clothes. By the time the police arrived, they found a half-naked Elvis clinging to the top of a shower stall. They escorted him to his car, which had been broken into and nearly stripped by the mob. Lovesick girls had written their names and telephone numbers in lipstick on his pink Cadillac. Some of his more destructive fans had carved their messages into the car's finish with nail files.

In 1956, Elvis' first single with RCA, "Heartbreak Hotel," was number one for eight weeks. That same year, his double-sided hit, "Hound Dog" and "Don't Be Cruel," topped the charts for a record eleven weeks. Elvis was considered such a threat to the morals of American youth that Ed Sullivan ordered his cameraman to shoot him only from the waist up. Preachers around the nation condemned Elvis as a spiritual degenerate and some radio stations banned his music.

Elvis always denied that his performing style was provocative. "I never feel sexy when I'm singing," he said. "If that was true, I'd be in some kind of institution as some kind of sex maniac."

The menace appeared to have ended when Elvis was drafted into the Army in March, 1958. Out of the public eye for two years, it was assumed that the Elvis Presley phenomenon was over. However, his popularity was so strong that when he was released from the service on March 5, 1960, it was as if he had never been away. He recorded "It's Now Or Never," based on the sixty-year-old Italian song, "O Sole Mio," and it sold more than twenty million records.

Women responded to Elvis as they did to no other performer. At his concerts, females screamed, fainted, and even wet their pants in excitement. Women may have swooned over Frank Sinatra, but they flipped over Elvis Presley. One female fan described him as "one big hunk of forbidden fruit."

Tuesday Weld certainly flipped over Elvis.

"I mean he was just drop dead!" she recalled in an interview years later. "Elvis was just so physically beautiful that even if he didn't have any talent...just his face...just his presence...I was totally in love with him. I was gaga about him."

Tuesday Weld was Elvis' first major romance after his return from the Army. They enjoyed taking long drives along the coast, sometimes going to Pacific Ocean Park. One of the things that Elvis found fascinating about Tuesday was her unpredictability. During one of their drives, Tuesday began throwing things, for no apparent reason, at people in passing cars. Occasionally, they went to greasy spoons to eat. After he got out of the service, Elvis had a weight problem—he was too thin. He loved to eat hamburgers, but his favorite meal was burned bacon, mashed potatoes, sauerkraut, and crowder peas, which he would mix up into a pile of mush before eating.

One of the couple's hangouts was an out-of-the-way rock and roll club in San Fernando named The Cross Bow. They would be secluded in the balcony where Elvis could view the dance floor but not be seen. They were rarely alone because Elvis was usually accompanied by his entourage. Tuesday and Elvis may have seemed like Romeo and Juliet on their balcony, but Elvis' extraordinary fame restricted their appearances in public. Tuesday was famous, but she was dating the most famous man in the world.

"He walked into a room and everything stopped," she remembered. "He knew what he had, and he didn't have to raise his voice; he didn't have to do anything except appear."

Tuesday also saw a more complex side of Elvis. "He was funny, charming, and complicated, but he didn't wear it on his sleeve."

Elvis was equally impressed with Tuesday, both physically and mentally. "That girl's not only got a good figure but a good mind," he said. "She gives a man the feeling that inside she seethes."

It was only natural that Twentieth Century Fox cast Elvis and Tuesday in a movie together. The film was called *Wild in the Country*. The title came from a line in Walt Whitman's *Leaves of Grass*. Producer Jerry Wald had been wanting to use the title for years.

Originally, *Wild in the Country* was to have been a serious film starring the French actress Simone Signoret. However, Signoret had recently won an Oscar for Best Actress for her performance in *Room at the Top*, and her asking price was too high for Wald. Nor was Elvis Presley the first choice for the role of Glenn Tyler. The role had been written for another teenage heartthrob, Fabian.

The director of *Wild in the Country* was Philip Dunne, son of humorist Finley Peter Dunne. He was one of Hollywood's most successful screenwriters. Dunne was a leading voice for liberal causes in Hollywood and wrote speeches for John F. Kennedy during the 1960 Presidential campaign.

The screenplay was written by Clifford Odets. During the 1930s, Odets had been the dominant voice in American theater. His most famous plays, *Golden Boy* and *The*

Country Girl, were adapted into films. Odets loosely based Elvis' character in the movie on novelist Thomas Wolfe.

Elvis welcomed the opportunity to play a serious role. As a child he had dreams of becoming a movie star. Like many young people in the 1950s, he identified strongly with James Dean. Elvis arrived in Hollywood to make his first movie just shortly after Dean was killed in an automobile accident, and he hoped to become the next James Dean. In fact, when director Robert Altman announced his intention to make a film about Dean's life, Elvis wanted to play Dean. The deal fell through, and the film was made as a documentary.

In 1958, Elvis was under serious consideration for the lead in *The Defiant Ones*, but the part went to Tony Curtis, one of Elvis' favorite actors. Elvis' famous pompadour had been inspired by the haircut Curtis wore in one of his early movies. His sideburns were a tribute to the silent screen lover, Rudolph Valentino.

One person who did not want to see Elvis star in a serious film was his manager, Colonel Tom Parker. Parker was a man with a mysterious past. Parker claimed he was born in West Virginia but, in reality, his real name was Andreas Van Kuijk, and he was born in Breda, Holland. He had come to America as a youth and earned his living in traveling carnivals where he gained a reputation as a masterful con man. Tales of his chicanery are legendary.

Parker sold foot-long hot dogs with no meat in the middle. He painted sparrows yellow and sold them as ca-

naries. Another of his tricks was to spread manure around
the tent and sell pony rides to people who, on seeing it,
didn't want to soil their shoes. His most famous sham was
his act which he called Tom Parker and His Dancing
Turkeys. The act consisted of a dozen turkeys dancing on
a sawdust covered table to the tune of "Turkey in the
Straw." What the audience didn't know was that the
Colonel placed an electric hot plate under the table to insure that his birds high stepped to the music.

Before he met Elvis, Parker managed country singers,
most notably Eddy Arnold. He had been bestowed the title
of honorary colonel in 1948 by Louisiana Governor
Jimmy Davis, a former country singer. Parker represented
only one client at a time, but he exacted a major fee for
his services. He took half of everything Elvis earned.

The Colonel believed the main purpose of Elvis making a movie was to record the soundtrack. He planned on
Elvis starring in three movies a year, each with enough
songs to fill an album. The formula was simple: put Elvis
in an exotic setting, add a gorgeous co-star, and some
songs.

Unlike Elvis' other movies, *Wild in the Country* was
supposed to be a dramatic picture, without songs. At the
Colonel's insistence, six songs were added (two songs
were later dropped). The songs included "Wild in the
Country," "I Slipped, I Stumbled, I Fell," "In My Way," and
"Husky Dusky Day." Director Philip Dunne threatened to
quit when he learned the musical numbers had been

added. Dunne was convinced that the role would establish Elvis Presley as a serious dramatic actor.

From then on, Elvis never was given the quality roles he wanted. His best opportunity occurred in 1961 when director Robert Wise considered him for the lead in the film adaptation of *West Side Story*. Wise's initial plan was to cast teen idols Fabian, Paul Anka, Frankie Avalon, and Bobby Darin as rival gang members. Once again Elvis was denied the chance to break out of his typecast role when Robert Wise decided to select more conventional actors for the parts.

"That should have been my part," Elvis said, when he saw *West Side Story*. "This guy they've got looks like a choir boy."

He was particularly incensed because the actor was not singing his own songs. "He's just mouthing it," Elvis snarled. "I could have sung them." Ironically, the actor Elvis was criticizing was Richard Beymer, Tuesday's former boyfriend.

Wild in the Country had a strong supporting cast which featured Hope Lange, Millie Perkins, John Ireland, and Gary Lockwood. It was filmed on location in the Napa Valley. Shooting began on November 11, 1960, in St. Helena, California.

Glenn Tyler (Elvis Presley) is a backwoods delinquent with a record of car theft and drunkenness. After being involved in a brawl, Glenn is put in the custody of his conniving uncle, Rolfe Braxton (William Mims). Rolfe's daughter, Noreen (Tuesday Weld), lives with her father and has a small baby. Glenn is told that her husband is overseas.

A psychologist, Irene Sperry (Hope Lange), takes an interest in Glenn and encourages him to write. Glenn learns that Noreen is an unwed mother and the father of her baby was a traveling salesman. Both Glenn and Noreen have a wild streak and they become lovers. Rolfe is eager to get his daughter married and offers to make Glenn a partner in his business if he will marry Noreen. Glenn refuses to be forced into marriage. The situation becomes more complicated when Glenn and Irene fall in love. Cliff Macy (Gary Lockwood) finds out that they spent a night together at a motel and tells his father, Phil (John Ireland), who is romantically involved with Irene.

Glenn decides to run off with Noreen. On the way out of town he encounters Cliff and strikes him. When Cliff dies, everyone assumes he died as a result of his fight with Glenn. Only his father and Irene know that Cliff had a serious heart condition which caused his death. Glenn is arrested for manslaughter. Irene, distraught because Glenn has been charged with murder, tries to commit suicide. Phil reveals his son's condition and Glenn is cleared of the charges. Irene recovers and convinces Glenn to go to college where he can develop his writing talent. Noreen accompanies him to the train station, promising she'll be waiting if he decides to renew their relationship.

Wild in the Country was a breakthrough film for Tuesday Weld because it gave her the opportunity to fully display her ability as a dramatic actress. She enjoyed portraying the bad girl Noreen because she was "lonely and desperate and drinks and has a baby, grasping for the impossible—happiness."

Philip Dunne said he had expected great performances from Tuesday Weld and Hope Lange, and he was pleased with Elvis' strong performance. Lange's performance was especially remarkable because she convincingly played the part of an older woman despite being only a year older than Elvis.

Considering the chaos which occurred behind the scenes, it was amazing that *Wild in the Country* was even completed. Tuesday caused a mild stir by insisting that her white Alsatian dog be allowed on the set in violation of the studio regulations. Millie Perkins broke her wrist in a scene where she slapped Elvis. During shooting Elvis was treated for painful boils on his rear.

These problems were minor compared to the obstacles encountered by the director. Clifford Odets' screenplay was twice as long as necessary and the studio refused to pay him for a rewrite. Elvis' salary represented half the film's budget and the studio was forced to cut corners wherever possible. With shooting about to begin, Dunne was given the unenviable task of editing and rewriting the entire script. Each night Dunne spent long hours finishing the next day's script.

After a month's shooting, Twentieth Century Fox president Spyros Skouras informed Dunne that he needed to complete the picture within a week. When Dunne protested that he couldn't possibly complete shooting in that time, the studio suggested that he cut out many of the remaining scenes. The problem was that the scenes Skouras recommended be cut were the pivotal ones in the film. Skouras compromised and gave Dunne twenty days to finish shooting. Dunne was able to wrap up shooting in nineteen days by having the cast work long hours of overtime.

Late one night he played a record of Bach's "Fifth Brandenburg Concerto" to get Elvis in the mood for an important love scene. Silent film directors used to play classical music on the set to get their stars in the proper mood. Dunne was surprised when the King of Rock and Roll told him he loved the music.

Just as production was about to end, the cast learned that Skouras had sold the studio's old back lot to developers in order to pay dividends to Twentieth Century Fox's stockholders. While the crew was trying to shoot the film's final scene at the railroad station, a Sherman tank was bulldozing some of the studio's most famous sets nearby. Despite these distractions, the train station scene was completed on schedule. As soon as filming was completed, the tank leveled the railroad depot as the cast and crew watched in silence.

Two endings were filmed. One ending had the Hope Lange character commit suicide in disgrace while the alternate ending had her survive. Both endings were tested, and the sneak preview audiences insisted that she live. The preview audiences unexpectedly jeered Elvis' songs and recommended they be dropped from the final cut but the studio ignored their suggestion. The songs were not among Elvis' best and none of them became hits.

Wild in the Country premiered in Memphis on June 15, 1961, and was distributed nationally a week later. The film proved to be a disappointment at the box office. Philip Dunne explained why he thought the film was commercially unsuccessful: "*Wild in the Country* fell between two stools. Audiences who might have liked Clifford Odets' drama wouldn't buy Elvis and his songs; Elvis fans were disappointed in a Presley picture which departed so radically from his usual song-and-sex comedy formula."

One person who did like the film was Elvis Presley. Elvis rarely liked his movies, but *Wild in the Country* became one of his favorites. He arranged for a private screening for his father, stepmother, and stepbrother. Elvis pointed out that he thought Hope Lange resembled his stepmother, Dee. His young stepbrother, Billy Stanley, had his eyes focused elsewhere. "I barely noticed Hope Lange," he wrote in his book, *Elvis, My Brother*. "That was because of Tuesday Weld. I was beginning to notice girls, though I'd never at that time admit it, and Tuesday Weld was a lot of girl to notice. I kept my eyes glued to the screen for every glimpse of Tuesday Weld."

Not everyone was so enamored of Tuesday Weld. Readers of *Teen* Magazine voted Tuesday Weld and Elvis Presley the Damp Raincoat Award, signifying the Most Disappointing Performers of 1961.

Many people still believed that Tuesday Weld would be the woman who would finally marry Elvis, but there were factors undermining their relationship. Shortly before she died in 1958, Elvis' mother, Gladys, had warned him about rushing into marriage. His mother remained the most important woman in his life, even after her death. No woman could live up to her in his eyes. Colonel Parker opposed the relationship with Tuesday because he believed if Elvis got married he would lose popularity with his female fans. When the Colonel demanded Elvis stop seeing Tuesday, the two men had a violent argument.

The tension caused by the relationship resulted in a violent encounter between Elvis and one of his longtime associates, Sonny West, a member of the Elvis Presley inner circle known as the Memphis Mafia.

According to West, Tuesday Weld visited Elvis at his home one evening. She brought along an attractive friend named Kay. Elvis began flirting with Kay, telling her how pretty she was and even kissing her. Meanwhile, West and another of Elvis' bodyguards were comparing the physical attributes of the two women. Sonny was asked, "If you had your pick, which would you take?" West didn't hesitate in replying, "Tuesday—she's got some body on her!"

Elvis overheard part of the conversation and demanded to know what they were talking about. When the
two men refused to answer, Elvis guessed the subject. It
was strictly prohibited for anyone to talk about a woman
he was involved with in his presence. Rather than submit
to the interrogation, Sonny West threatened to quit. As
West tried to leave the room, Elvis grabbed a Coke bottle as though he might strike him. "You're not quitting because you're fired!" Elvis shouted. Out of control, Elvis
punched West in the jaw but the blow didn't even faze the
powerful bodyguard. Eventually, the two men patched up
their differences and West remained a close companion to
Elvis for many years.

Tuesday's mother was often critical of Tuesday's dates
and even Elvis didn't escape her displeasure. She was waiting one evening when Elvis brought Tuesday home at 3:30
in the morning.

"Don't you know she has a 9:00 a.m. studio call?" Mrs.
Weld asked.

"Mine's even earlier," Elvis replied.

It became apparent that Tuesday was not going to be
the woman to marry Elvis. The break-up was gradual, and
they remained friends after their romance was over. Elvis
had a special quality which allowed him to stay on good
terms with his past loves. He was old fashioned and insisted that his future wife not have her own career. Elvis
liked to have complete control of his women. Tuesday was

a free spirit who would never allow herself to be domi-
nated—even by Elvis.

Elvis was always cautious with women, afraid they
might be after his money. He claimed he could tell after
the third date if the woman was interested in him or his
wealth. By his own admission he had relationships with
more than one thousand women, probably a conservative
estimate. Elvis could have any woman he wanted, but he
was always looking for that special girl he would marry.

That girl turned out to be Priscilla Beaulieu, whom he
met when he was stationed in Germany. She was only
fourteen years old then they met, but Elvis told a friend
that he knew immediately she was the one. Priscilla was
aware that there were many women in Elvis' life. She was
especially jealous of his relationship with Tuesday. Elvis
convinced her that the romance was a ploy dreamed up by
the studio's publicity department. On Christmas Eve,
1966, four years after Priscilla moved into Graceland,
Elvis proposed to her. They were married at Milton Prell's
Aladdin Hotel in Las Vegas on May 1, 1967.

Years later Tuesday Weld reflected on Elvis. "I don't
know what he felt about me. But I know he liked me. He
wasn't in love with me, and in actuality, I don't know if I
was in love with him. But who wasn't in love with him?"

When asked to describe Elvis, Tuesday replied, "Dynamite! Real dynamite!"

Chapter 6

The Next Marilyn Monroe

Tuesday Weld was suddenly a hot property in Hollywood. A *Time* magazine reporter wrote at the time: "In Hollywood's scheme of things, Tuesday Weld ranks higher than Joan of Arc." Twentieth Century Fox producer Robert Blees predicted that Tuesday was on the verge of becoming a major dramatic actress. "She's grown out of her past. Some day she'll do *The Jean Harlow Story* and tear your heart out."

Twentieth Century Fox signed Tuesday to a lucrative six picture deal. "It cost them plenty," Tuesday bragged. Plenty amounted to $35,000 per picture. To supplement her income, she raised pedigree poodles which she sold for princely prices.

Even while filming *Wild in the Country*, Tuesday Weld began work on another movie, *Return to Peyton Place*. For a time her schedule was juggled to allow her to work on both films. Jerry Wald, who produced both *Wild in the Country* and *Return to Peyton Place*, said of Tuesday, "She's a colorful girl of many sides who's gone through the publicity orbit and is now in focus. She has depth and sensitivity."

Return to Peyton Place was a sequel to the enormously successful *Peyton Place*. Based on the bestselling novel by Grace Metalious, *Peyton Place* told the story of the residents of a small New England town whose placid exterior concealed adultery, incest, and murder. The name Peyton Place became synonymous with small-town hypocrisy.

The cast of *Return to Peyton Place* included Carol Lynley, Eleanor Parker, Jeff Chandler, and Mary Astor. The producers had tried to sign the original stars, without success. Lana Turner, who played Constance Mackenzie, was replaced by Eleanor Parker after she demanded that her salary be tripled. Diane Varsi, who played Allison Mackenzie, had walked out of the studio, saying she was leaving Hollywood forever. Her replacement was Carol Lynley. Tuesday Weld played Selena Cross, a role originated by Hope Lange, her co-star in *Wild in the Country*.

Reportedly, Joan Crawford had been first choice for the role of Constance Mackenzie, but she backed out at the last minute. In *Mommie Dearest*, the best-selling account of their turbulent relationship, her daughter, Christina, wrote that Crawford was angry at the studio because Christina had been given a role in *Wild in the Country*. For whatever reason, Christina's contract was soon dropped by Twentieth Century Fox.

Return to Peyton Place was directed by Jose Ferrer, who won an Academy Award for Best Actor for his performance in *Cyrano de Bergerac* in 1950. His trademark was his magnificent, deep speaking voice. Ferrer became one of the first stars to go behind the camera as a director. Prior to *Return to Peyton Place*, Ferrer had directed five films, most notably *The Shrike* and *The Great Man*.

Shooting for the film was scheduled to begin in the summer of 1960 in Camden, Maine. Strikes by the Screen Actors' Guild and Writers' Guild delayed the production by months. As a result the storyline was changed from a summer to a winter setting. Tuesday's love interest in the film, who was originally a summer stock teacher, became a ski instructor. Exterior shots were filmed in Mammoth, California.

The film opens with young Allison Mackenzie (Carol Lynley) anxiously awaiting word concerning publication of her first novel. She receives a phone call from New York publisher, Lewis Jackman (Jeff Chandler), who expresses interest in publishing the book. Allison hurries to her mother's dress shop to tell her the good news.

Working in the dress shop is Allison's best friend, Selena Cross (Tuesday Weld), the town's outcast. Selena was socially ostracized by the community when she murdered her stepfather after he brutally raped her. Although she was acquitted at her trial, she was never forgiven by the self-righteous citizens of Peyton Place.

Especially hostile toward her is the town's matriarch, Roberta Carter (Mary Astor). She dislikes Selena because her son, Ted (Brett Halsey), had stood by her at the trial, arousing suspicions that they were having an affair. Roberta is shocked when Ted brings home a bride, an Italian model named Rafaella (Luciana Paluzzi). The possessive Roberta decides to invite Selena to her home, hoping the visit might cause the newlyweds to break up.

Selena soon realizes that she is being used by Roberta and speeds away in her car. On her way home, she nearly has an accident with the town's new ski instructor, Lars (Gunnar Hellstrom). She is initially rude to Lars but finds herself attracted to him. Later, she collides with him on the ski slopes. Lars jokes, "You have the soul of an assassin."

In New York, Lewis Jackman personally assists Allison in the editing of her novel, *Samuel's Castle*. Jackson conducts a media blitz to make Allison Mackenzie America's new literary sweetheart. Allison falls in love with the older married man.

The novel is a thinly veiled portrait of the residents of Peyton Place. Many of the townspeople are outraged, particularly Roberta Carter, who thinks the book is trash, and Allison's mother, Constance (Eleanor Parker), whose affair with a married man is revealed. At the lodge, Lars reads the first chapter of the novel to Selena. It is obvious to both of them that one of the book's main characters, Sarah Crane, is based on Selena. Lars reads the description of her: "Sarah, with her breathtaking broad open face, full ripe mouth, great blue laughing eyes trimmed by long silken lashes."

Selena urges Lars to continue reading chapter two. The chapter begins ominously as Sarah is described as being "too well developed for her age." Lars begins reading the graphic description of Sarah being raped by her stepfather. Before he is able to finish the passage, Selena grabs the book and throws it in the fire. Lars demands to know what happened, prompting Selena to scream: "You want to know all the dirty, perverted details of the sex act." She tells him how she was raped by her stepfather when she was thirteen years old and that she bludgeoned him to death with a log. Selena loses control and strikes Lars with a poker, knocking him unconscious. She flees through the snow and disappears.

Allison's stepfather, Mike Rossi (Robert Sterling), is the principal of the local high school. When he attempts to place Allison's book in the school library, the school board threatens to dismiss him. A town meeting is called to decide his fate. Roberta Carter is humiliated when her son steps forth and defends the book. At the climactic moment, Selena enters the town hall. "You made me feel what happened was my fault," she said. "You made me feel dirty and unwanted." She pleads that Allison's book be admitted to the library and the townspeople agree.

During the filming of *Return to Peyton Place*, rumors of a feud between Tuesday and Carol Lynley surfaced. Lynley, one of the hottest starlets in Hollywood, announced she was retiring to devote full-time to her marriage to Mike Selsman. Tuesday suggested that the retirement was just a publicity stunt. The "feud," real or manufactured, was soon forgotten.

Return to Peyton Place was an important film for Tuesday, marking her transition from teenage to mature roles. Despite her fine performances, she disliked watching herself on the screen. "I hate to see my rushes," she admitted. "I always think I look horrible in movies. I haven't seen my last five, but I think I'll look at *Return to Peyton Place* and *Wild in the Country* so I can compare them."

Tuesday's next film, *Bachelor Flat*, was a return to comedy. The film starred her ex-boyfriend, Richard Beymer, Oscar winner Celeste Holm, and gap-toothed British comedian Terry-Thomas. Initially, Thomas was intimidated by Tuesday. He wrote in his autobiography: "What I remember most about *Bachelor Flat* was the extraordinary behavior of Tuesday Weld. She earned the distinction of being the most frightening person I had ever come across—a title she still holds."

He was particularly appalled by her reckless driving. "I thought she lived the most dangerous life—quite shocking! She used to drive a car as long as the Queen Mary and park it anywhere, whether there was a vacant spot or not. She would drive up on the pavement, unconcerned whether or not it was blocking someone's access. She would just leave the car, often with the engine running, then gaily walk away."

The director of *Bachelor Flat* was Frank Tashlin. A former cartoonist, he directed many of Jerry Lewis' early films, including *Artists and Models* and *Geisha Boy*, and was an important influence on the comedian's subsequent work as a director. Jean-Luc Godard, one of the founders of French New Wave cinema and director of such classics as *Breathless* and *Weekend*, hailed Tashlin as the "vanguard of the modern comedy style in film."

Terry-Thomas played Bruce Patterson, a professor of archaeology at a California university. The professor is engaged to Helen (Celeste Holm), a woman his own age. He is staying at her beachfront home while she is away on business. Unexpectedly, Helen's daughter, Libby Bushmill (Tuesday Weld), arrives home from college. Helen has not told Bruce that she has a grown daughter because she is sensitive about her age.

Libby is surprised to discover Bruce in her mother's house. She decides to conceal her true identity. She tells Bruce she is a juvenile delinquent on the run from the police and that she needs "a good hideout until the heat dies down." He reluctantly agrees to let her stay temporarily.

The next morning Libby makes breakfast while dressed in a bra, blue shorts, and white high heels. She does a seductive dance while drinking a Coke. Mike (Richard Beymer), a medical student who lives in a trailer next door, is immediately attracted to her and suspicious of her story.

Professor Patterson decides the right thing to do is to turn Libby over to the police. He leaves her there, but Mike is waiting to take her home on his motorbike. That night, the guilt-ridden Bruce has nightmares. He dreams that Libby escapes from prison and promises to rub him out. Libby, dressed like a gun moll, smoking a cigar and wielding a shotgun, captures Bruce. Just as she is about to shoot him, he wakes up. He is startled when he sees Libby in striped pajamas which resemble prison garb.

Helen arrives home and Libby helps to clear up the misunderstanding. Mike realizes that Libby is Helen's daughter. "You're beautiful, just like her," he says.

By the end of the filming, Terry-Thomas had come to respect Tuesday as a professional, whose nonconformity never interfered with her work. "Tuesday was a good performer," he observed. "When acting she was not difficult as were many Hollywood stars. It was just off stage that Tuesday did not conform."

Co-starring with Richard Beymer fueled speculation that they might rekindle their romance. Beymer had overcome his earlier reluctance to act in another film with Tuesday, but now their relationship was strictly on screen. When Beymer was asked if he was dating her, he replied,

"Gee, no. I thought everybody knew she goes steady with Gary Lockwood."

Gary Lockwood was a handsome twenty-four year old actor who had been a football star at UCLA until he was suspended following a fight in the locker room which sent a teammate to the hospital. Because of his athletic ability, Lockwood was hired as a stuntman in the basketball film, *Tall Story*, starring Anthony Perkins. Director Joshua Logan rewarded him with a small part as a Russian basketball player.

He had met Tuesday during the filming of *Wild in the Country*. At the time, Lockwood was dating Christina Crawford. "It wasn't love at first sight," he said. "We fell in love gradually." Lockwood was attracted by Tuesday's appearance, but he was even more attracted to her intelligence.

Lockwood said, "With Tuesday, love isn't a four-letter word. It's the whole alphabet. Ours is not a love affair—it's an adventure."

For a time they were inseparable. They especially enjoyed outdoor activities such as swimming and tennis. Tuesday was an excellent swimmer and would swim in the ocean while her dog, Wolf, ran barking on the beach. Gary complimented her on her athletic ability and taught her to water ski. They also shared cultural interests. They attended a performance of the visiting Moiseyev Ballet and loved it.

When they were together, it was if no one else was present. When filming was completed on *Bachelor Flat*, a party was thrown for the cast. Tuesday and Gary were so immersed in conversation that when Terry-Thomas tried to break in they didn't even notice him. The fan magazines wrote of Lockwood: "All his nights are Tuesday."

Their motto was: "Life's too short to have a terrible time." Lockwood admitted that he had never met a girl like Tuesday. After only three dates he realized she was the only girl he ever wanted to see. He said, "I'm a floater. I can be attracted for a couple of weeks and boom, a girl does something wrong, she complains about my profane language, and we've had it. I've never had a rapport with a woman like I have now with Tuesday."

Tuesday was attracted to Lockwood's manliness and take-charge attitude. She explained his appeal: "It's hard to describe. It has nothing to do with his big football muscles. You respect him for himself. A lot of guys will let you have too much latitude, let you have a lot of string. Let's say that Gary's string is very taut. He won't stand for any nonsense."

Some people believed Gary Lockwood had Tuesday Weld on a string. In October, 1961, *Photoplay* magazine quoted Tuesday as saying, "I've finally met my master."

The couple spent a lot of time at the beach, near the oceanside home of one of Gary's friends. They could be seen in places like Malibu, Venice, Playa Del Ray, and Portuguese Beach. They enjoyed watching movies at the Village Theatre in Westwood and taking late night drives along the beach in Gary's red Corvette. One day at the beach they had an argument. Tuesday walked away. Rather than ask her to stop as most other men would have done, Lockwood let her go. She came back to him.

The press speculated that they might get married at any time. Tuesday hinted that she was considering getting married on her eighteenth birthday. She soon dispelled any rumors that she was in a hurry to get to the altar. "It's not that I'm afraid of responsibility—I've had that since I was three. But if someone gives me a part in a show in Afghanistan, I want to be free to take it. If I want to dance barefoot on Sunset Boulevard at midnight, I don't want to worry about what anyone else would think."

At Tuesday's eighteenth birthday party, her mother served a gourmet meal. Gary Lockwood was among the half dozen guests. He brought her two presents: a bright orange cardigan and a pair of hand-made earrings. For his birthday she bought him a green sweater.

Lockwood said that Tuesday always bragged that she never wanted people to understand her. He noted that unlike the Thalia Menninger role she created on television, she was not a material girl. "Tuesday's not concerned with material things. She's smart enough to realize that happiness is better than nonsense. I've seen her have more fun on fifty cents than anyone else could on fifty dollars."

Tuesday's one extravagance was automobiles. "Really, the only thing I've seen her flip for is cars," Lockwood said. She loved to take long drives in Gary's little red Corvette. Sometimes she would drive her silver Thunderbird so her dog, Wolf, could sit in the back seat.

At the time, Gary Lockwood was starring on an adventure television series on ABC called *Follow the Sun*. Tuesday guest starred in an episode entitled "The Highest Wall" in which she played a Philadelphia Main Line debutante.

Tuesday Weld and Gary Lockwood co-starred in the pilot for the television series, *Bus Stop*. *Bus Stop* was based on a William Inge play which was made into a 1956 movie. Tuesday played a waitress named Cherie, a role made famous by Marilyn Monroe in the film version. The episode was directed by Don Siegel, a first-rate director who had made the classic horror film, *Invasion of the Body Snatchers*. Siegel was extremely pleased with Tuesday's performance. He said, "I'd say she took a long look at herself and realized that Tuesday Weld could either become a Hollywood joke or a synonym for an actress. She reached deep into her instincts and pulled out her best performance." *Bus Stop* producer Roy Huggins was equally enthusiastic in his praise: "Tuesday couldn't have been better." Her co-star Gary Lockwood agreed, "There's a tremendous love affair that goes on between Tuesday and the camera."

Bus Stop went on the air as a regular series on ABC in October, 1961, but neither Tuesday Weld nor Gary Lockwood were in the cast. The series, which starred Joan Freeman and Rhodes Reason, was canceled after five months, partly because of a disturbing episode which featured Fabian as a psychopath. The episode was so controversial that it was cited in Congressional hearings investigating violence on television.

Tuesday and Gary often had spirited conversations. Lockwood found her to be highly opinionated and surprisingly mature. "This girl has something to say on every subject," he marvelled. "We may go to war on it, but that's okay too. When we disagree, she'll read up on the subject and come back recharged…She thinks well, she has terrific instincts. She's curious about life and longs for experience. There probably aren't twenty-five girls her age in this country who are as mature as Tuesday…She's the least confused actress in the business, her values are absolutely sound."

Both Tuesday and Gary had tempers and were subject to sudden mood swings. He was attracted to her mercurial nature. "She has a wonderful personality, she's stormy like I am," he said. It was their relationship which became increasingly stormy. The fan magazines carried stories about their "tortured romance." *Photoplay* wrote of Gary Lockwood: "One moment his nights are all Tuesday, the next his nights are all hell." They broke up for two months, then reconciled.

In December, 1962, Hedda Hopper reported in her column that Tuesday Weld had accidentally hit Gary Lockwood over the head with a telephone, knocking him unconscious for several minutes. Lockwood was a muscular athlete and a karate expert, but he always seemed to come out second best in their fights. The most violent incident occurred when Tuesday tried to run Gary down with her car. He saved himself by jumping on the hood. Tuesday sped down Sunset Boulevard with Gary clinging to the hood while pleading for his life through the windshield.

Actor Ryan O'Neal commented, "Tuesday did some wild things and screwed up many, many guys. She's highly sexual. It's what makes her interesting on the screen."

Tuesday lamented her difficulty in maintaining a lasting relationship. "It's never satisfactory. Either the man is able to keep you happy sexually and has no intellectual quality; or he's very intellectual and not good at carrying on a satisfactory sexual relationship."

Her career was going smoother than her love life. By her own admission, she earned $126,000 as an eighteen-year old. She owned six automobiles in one year, beginning with a silver T-Bird and ending with a white Cadillac convertible. She also inherited a sizable estate of stocks and bonds from her paternal grandmother. This income took some of the pressure off and gave her the luxury of being selective in choosing her acting assignments. Her mother said, "The inheritance will save her from becoming dependent on the whims of Hollywood, which no girl should ever be subjected to."

Between films, Tuesday was a popular guest on television, commanding as much as ten thousand dollars for an appearance. She was on the *Red Skelton Show*, *77 Sunset Strip*, *Cimarron Strip*, *The Millionaire*, *The Dinah Shore Chevy Show*, *Zane Grey Theatre*, the *Naked City*, and *The Dick Powell Show*.

In 1962, she guest-starred on *Adventures in Paradise*, a series set in Tahiti and based on an idea by author James Michener. The episode, "The Velvet Trap," was directed by Mitchell Leisen, a respected veteran who had directed the noted screwball comedies, *Easy Living* and *Midnight*. Tuesday played Gloria Dannora, the daughter of a mobster on-the-run. *Adventures in Paradise* star Gardner McKay said, "Tuesday is a delightful youngster until the moment you start working with her—then she's a lot of woman and a real actress."

One of her memorable appearances was on the CBS dramatic series, *Route 66*. The episode, entitled "Love Is a Skinny Kid," co-starred Cloris Leachman and was aired on April 6, 1962. Tuesday played Miriam, a mysterious young woman who returns as a social outcast. She wears a Japanese mask to conceal her identity. Appearing in a small role was a little-known young actor named Burt Reynolds.

TV Guide noted her return to television in a feature article titled "The Face That Launched a Thousand Column Items." In 1962, Tuesday agreed to make a guest appearance as Thalia Menninger on *The Many Loves of Dobie Gillis*. Two years had gone by since she had left the show. Dobie graduated from high school and was now enrolled in college. In an episode called "Birth of a Salesman," Thalia had become a salesperson and tried to talk Dobie into dropping out of college to join her business.

The cast of Dobie Gillis presented Tuesday with a cake on her return. The show's creator, Max Shulman, found Tuesday to be a completely different person than the fifteen-year-old girl who had played Thalia during the first season. "This was an elegant Tuesday we'd never seen before—a real professional, hair up, wearing a smart business suit. And she knew her lines. In the old days she never used to know line one." Director Rod Amateau recalled, "She was precocious, professional, and rightfully self-assured."

Tuesday was approached about starring in her own television sit-com. She made a pilot for Desilu called *Working Girl* in which she portrayed a working girl in New York City. The premise seemed promising but the series was not picked up by the networks for the 1962 fall season.

Tuesday was always mentioned among Hollywood sex symbols. She was compared to Elizabeth Taylor, another child star who had developed into a sex symbol. She was touted as the sexiest teenager since Liz.

Leon Shamroy, the cinematographer for Weld in *Rally Round the Flag, Boys!* and for Taylor in *Cleopatra*, believed Tuesday had all the qualifications to become the next Hollywood sex goddess. "To become a sex goddess in motion pictures, a girl must first of all be photogenically revealing. Second, she has to stimulate the men in the audience without antagonizing the women. For my money, the next Hollywood sex goddess could be Tuesday Weld. Tuesday has all the attributes. She's only nineteen and much smarter than Marilyn ever was. She's got as many curves as a scenic railway, and most important of all, she comes across on film."

Elizabeth Taylor was constantly in the headlines because of her marital problems, and the press predicted a similar fate for Tuesday. One Hollywood newspaperman wrote: "Like Liz, Tuesday will probably have too many lovers, too many husbands, and too much heartache before she's twenty-five."

Then there were the endless comparisons with Marilyn Monroe. It was no secret that the studio was looking for a replacement for Monroe, who was in her mid-thirties and was becoming increasingly unreliable. When Monroe was found dead in her home on August 5, 1962, the search began for her successor. Tuesday Weld was the leading candidate. One executive at Twentieth Century Fox was quoted as saying, "I hope this kid [Tuesday Weld] makes it as a replacement for Marilyn Monroe; if she doesn't, I don't know anyone else in this town who can."

Numerous actresses, ranging from Stella Stevens to Jayne Mansfield, were touted as "the next Marilyn Monroe," but Tuesday, alone, seemed to possess the qualities to make her the logical replacement. Author Lloyd Shearer made a strong case for Tuesday: "Here is a lovely, young, chameleon-eyed blond, 5 feet 4, 110 pounds, with a 36-23-34 figure, firm, well-toned, beautifully shaped. She boasts Freudian allure and an ample bosom, two of the prime requisites of the typical American sex symbol. As a bonus, Tuesday can act. She's been working ever since she was three-and-a-half, takes direction quickly, easily, and perceptively."

Tuesday was not interested in becoming the next blonde bombshell.

"I'm a good actress," she said. "I can play more than sex-bait or the girl who arouses wolf whistles. I've been described as a kook and an oddball and an erupting volcano, but I'm none of those. I'm trying to improve all the time. I don't want Hollywood to treat me the way it treated Marilyn Monroe. She hung around this town, wasting the best years of her life trying to get jobs... She told everyone she was serious about her work, but producers would look at her figure and they would never believe her. Somehow a girl who bulges in the right places is never considered a serious artist in Hollywood."

Tuesday retreated to her home in Malibu. She expressed the desire to "go away and grow up." She vowed to "condense all of her energy and frustrations." "It has been so long since I really worked at something."

Chapter 7

The New Tuesday

Tuesday Weld was at a crossroads in her career. At twenty, she was getting too old for the sex kitten roles. Like Marilyn Monroe, she wanted to be given the opportunity to become a serious actress. Her uncertainty was reflected in her own self-appraisal. "When I look in the mirror, sometimes I see the mature actress I'd like to be. Sometimes I see the child-woman they say I am. Sometimes I see the badly spoiled little brat I might well be. And sometimes I see nothing at all."

She remarked, "All of life is a turning point."

Her next film, *Soldier in the Rain*, was certainly a turning point in Hollywood's perception of Tuesday as an actress. She still had the reputation of being difficult, which caused producers to be hesitant about hiring her. Martin Jurow, the producer of *Soldier in the Rain*, explained he was pleasantly surprised by her reliability. "In the past, you were concerned whether or not she would carry out her assignment. In *Soldier*, there was not a moment in which she was late or failed to relate to her performance."

Actually, there was one relapse. She played hooky on wardrobe test day. To cover her tracks, her press agent planted a phony story in the newspaper that her dog had been run over by a car.

Blake Edwards, who produced and co-authored *Soldier in the Rain*, remembered Tuesday from *High Time*, which he directed. The director, Ralph Nelson, was known for his ability to draw the best performance from an actor. During his career, he directed both Sidney Poitier and Cliff Robertson to Best Actor Oscars. The strong cast included Steve McQueen, Jackie Gleason, Tom Poston, and Tony Bill.

Steve McQueen was one of the hottest young actors in Hollywood. As a youth, he had been involved with street gangs and spent two years in a California reform school. Before he became an actor, he spent several years working a variety of odd jobs including being an errand boy in a brothel, a carnival barker, a lumberjack, a ballpoint pen salesman, and finally, a television repairman.

While working as a TV repairman in Greenwich Village, he met performers who encouraged him to try acting. His big break occurred in 1958 when he was cast in the role of bounty hunter Josh Randall, in the television Western, *Wanted Dead or Alive*. The program was a Top Ten hit and McQueen became one of the first anti-hero stars. He made a smooth transition from television to films, starring in such box office hits as *The Magnificent Seven* and *The Great Escape*. He accepted the role of Eustie Clay in *Soldier in the Rain* because he didn't want to be typecast and wanted a lighter role to display his versatility.

Tuesday's other co-star, comedian Jackie Gleason, also made his name in television as Ralph Kramden in the sit-com, *The Honeymooners*. Like McQueen, he also made the successful transition to films. The "Great One" earned an Oscar nomination in 1961 for his performance as Min-nesota Fats in *The Hustler*.

Soldier in the Rain, a service comedy with serious over-tones, was based on a novel by William Goldman, who once said of Hollywood: "Nobody here knows anything." Eustis Clay (Steve McQueen) is a supply sergeant who is considering leaving the Army at the end of his tour of duty. He hopes to go into business with his best friend, Master Sergeant Maxwell Slaughter (Jackie Gleason). Sergeant has all the comforts of home in his office (air conditioner, stereo equipment, and a Pepsi machine which only works for him) and is not so eager to leave the security of the ser-vice. Slaughter dreams of retiring to a white beached Pa-cific island where the "people are friendly and all the girls are slim, with long legs and round firm breasts that tilt up."

Eustis' latest scheme concerns Private Jerry Meltzer (Tony Bill), who claims he can run a three-minute mile. Eustis takes him out on a deserted road at dusk to time him. As he drives alongside the runner, he doesn't notice a car racing up behind him. The cars collide, knocking both vehicles off the road. As Eustis climbs from the wreckage he notices one of the occupants of the other car, Bobby Jo Pepperdine (Tuesday Weld), calmly putting on lipstick as if nothing had happened. "Well, Eustis, what's new?" she asks.

Eustis arranges for a date between Sergeant Slaughter and Bobby Jo. Their mutual dislike is evident when they're introduced. Bobby Jo greets Maxwell by saying, "Hi, Fatty." When Eustis comments that Bobby Jo is very bright for her age, Maxwell replies, "She's an imbecile." Angrily, Bobby Jo calls Maxwell unflattering names such as "Blimp Face," "Balloon Head," "Jelly Belly," and "Blubber Mouth."

After Sergeant Slaughter apologizes, she reluctantly agrees to go to a carnival with him. He buys her some cotton candy which he calls "a gossamer fantasy, the stuff that dreams are made of." Bobby Jo attempts to impress Maxwell by mentioning she's a homeroom monitor at school. "A terrible responsibility," she admits. Her main ambitions are to buy a new wardrobe and a 21-inch television set.

The pair encounters another sergeant who threatens Bobby Jo for breaking a date with him. Sergeant Slaughter clamps a bearhug on him and makes him apologize.

Bobby Jo is thrilled that two men are fighting over her. "You were like Randolph Scott in the movies—a fat Randolph Scott," she tells Maxwell. When fireworks are set off, she remarks, "I think fireworks are the saddest things in the world—the way they disappear. They should make them so they just sit up there all night."

Eustis, Maxwell, and Bobby Jo play a round of golf. Bobby Jo walks the course in high heels, teeing up the ball for her "baby boyfriend." "I'm so happy," she says. "It feels like Saturday and I know it's only Tuesday, so I know Saturday's still coming."

The round is interrupted when Eustis learns that his beloved hunting dog, Donald, has died. That night, he is taunted by sadistic Sergeant Priest (Ed Nelson) at a bar. Sergeant Slaughter arrives and dispatches the two MPs but suffers a heart attack from the strain. When Sergeant Slaughter dies, Eustis decides to reenlist.

The performances in *Soldier in the Rain* were solid, particularly those of Tuesday Weld and Jackie Gleason. Bosley Crowther, film critic of *The New York Times*, wrote: "Tuesday Weld does very nicely in the almost impossible role of an illiterate Southern schoolgirl who takes a shine to Mr. Gleason." Judith Crist in the *New York Herald Tribune* described Tuesday as "a lovely blonde who portrays a teenage submoron to perfection."

Steve McQueen was so impressed by Tuesday's performance that he called her "the best actress I've worked with." Producer Martin Jurow predicted Tuesday would become a major star. "She has a tough exterior at times and yet in her eyes there is always a remarkable compassion. Carole Lombard had that quality and I think Tuesday has the capacity to grow and mature and become an interesting leading woman. She can be a true star."

The film received mixed reviews. It was hurt at the box office by the unfortunate timing of its release. *Soldier in the Rain* opened on November 27, 1963, five days after the Kennedy assassination. American audiences, in mourning for their fallen president, were not in the mood for comedy.

Tuesday's press agents decided to launch a publicity campaign to introduce the "New Tuesday Weld." They promised a new and improved Tuesday, with a stronger character, more pleasing personality, and better attitude. Tuesday would get up at 5:00 a.m. to accommodate interviewers. Louella Parsons, one of her harshest critics, told Tuesday, "You've turned out to be a very respectable character." Director Ted Post said, "There's always been a deep, serious vein in this girl and it's coming out now."

On July 26, 1963, *Life* magazine carried a feature article entitled "The Transformation of Tuesday." The three-page pictorial showed Tuesday at Palisades Park with her two young nieces. The article suggested that Tuesday was recapturing her lost childhood. "For most of her short life Tuesday has been far too old…She's begun to act nineteen going on twelve."

The Saturday Evening Post, the magazine which was then synonymous with American family values, ran a feature on Tuesday which said she was working hard to erase her oddball reputation. Tuesday admitted, "Let's face it. I had the reputation of being a kook, a sexy, flimsy broad."

Unfortunately, the description of her home contained in the article did little to dispel her image. Ants swarmed over the remains of a barbecue sandwich which was left on a TV snack table. When Tuesday attempted to make toast for breakfast, the charred pieces of bread popped out of the toaster onto the floor. To create the proper atmosphere during the interview, Tuesday played the soundtrack from *Mondo Cane*.

Finally, Tuesday had enough of the charade. She told her publicists, "I'm just not going along with this kind of nonsense. I had a terrible reputation and I guess that I still do." Tuesday claimed she was immune to anything the press wrote about her. "I'm not bothered by what I read about myself anymore," she said.

On April 13, 1964, Tuesday presented the Oscar for sound effects at the Academy Awards ceremonies held at the Santa Monica Auditorium. Her hairstyle that evening was inspired by the bouffant style popularized by Jackie Kennedy. As she was reading the nominees, her bouffant hairstyle collapsed and fell in her face. The embarrassing moment became one of the most famous bloopers in Academy Awards history.

Tuesday continued to make frequent guest appearances on television. She guest starred on *The Eleventh Hour*, *The Greatest Show on Earth*, and the DuPont Play of the Month's presentation of "The Legend of Lylah Clare."

One of her most noteworthy television appearances was on an episode of *The Fugitive* entitled "Dark Corner" which aired on November 10, 1964. Tuesday played Mattie Braydon, a blind sculptress. Mattie helps Richard Kimble (David Janssen) find refuge from the police. She asks Kimble to model for her but when he rebuffs her romantic advances, she turns against him.

Kimble is unaware that Mattie has a dark past. She became blind at the age of eight after she tried to push her sister, Clara, off a ledge and fell instead. Mattie decides to exact her revenge by seducing her sister's boyfriend, Bob. When her father becomes suspicious, Mattie backs over him in the family station wagon. She blames the "accident" on a gear which has been slipping. Richard Kimble forces Mattie to confess to her crime. As the police arrive, Mattie, still suffering from hysterical blindness, regains her sight.

Weld's performance, which foreshadowed her role as a murderess in *Pretty Poison*, was a wonderfully subtle portrait of evil. In an interview shortly after the episode aired, she expressed her difficulty in understanding the character's motivation. "If a Method acting school ever gets a script of 'Dark Corner,' it will set their curriculum back a dozen years. A Method actor would have to run quite a gamut to portray Mattie's emotions, and ask herself quite a few questions, like, 'At the start, am I really a nice person? Do I fall in love with Kimble? Do I change because he rejects me? Would his rejection change me into a vicious person gradually or rapidly?'"

Another interesting project for television failed to materialize. Tuesday was scheduled to co-star with Robert Culp on *The Dick Powell Theater* in an episode entitled "The Gunfighter." The episode was to be directed by Sam Peckinpah, who had established his reputation in television before making a spectacular film directorial debut in 1962 with the classic western, *Ride the High Country*.

The storyline concerned a fast gun champion played by Culp who goes berserk after losing a contest in Las Vegas and goes on a killing spree before committing suicide. Culp, who would later co-star with Bill Cosby on the long-running action series, *I Spy*, believed the script was the best he had ever read. To prepare for the role, Culp had performed gun tricks at state fairs and on the rodeo circuit. The subject matter was mature for its time and "The Gunfighter" would have been an intriguing production. Unfortunately, the program's host, Dick Powell, died of cancer and his show went off the air before the episode could be filmed.

Tuesday did guest star on the premier episode of a CBS series called *Mr. Broadway* starring Craig Stevens. The episode, "Keep an Eye on Emily," was shown on September 26, 1964, and featured Stevens as Mike Bell, a public relations man in New York who would do anything to maintain his client's reputations. Garson Kanin, the multitalented producer, director, and writer, was amazed by how Tuesday had gotten her act together. "What I ran into was one of the most organized young creatures I have ever encountered anywhere," Kanin said. "She is not like anyone I've ever known. She's original and absolutely unique, not a poseur, not a phony. She has tremendous vitality, magnetism, and that best of all qualities—real mystery. I would buy stock in the Tuesday Weld Corporation if it were for sale."

As far as the motion picture industry was concerned, Tuesday's stock was down. She hadn't made a film in nearly two years. One casting director suggested that the problem might be Tuesday's disposition. "If only she would smile more often, Tuesday would get more jobs. Sure, she's sexy, but she's also sullen. She gives one the feeling that she considers life a burden rather than a joy. No one had a more terrible youth than Marilyn Monroe. Yet she always managed to smile. This kid doesn't. The minute she does, the sky is the limit for her because in addition to sex appeal she's got real talent, and that's an unbeatable combination."

Tuesday was doing little to promote her career. She said, "I have never been ambitious, so I don't go out and seek acting jobs and, since everyone in Hollywood thought

I was crazy, they weren't beating down my door with job offers anyway."

In 1964, Tuesday nearly landed the starring role in a British production, *Of Human Bondage*, Somerset Maugham's tale of a doctor's infatuation with a waitress. The film was to star Kim Novak and be directed by Henry Hathaway. Both actress and director had the reputation of being difficult, and they were completely incompatible. Novak walked off the set, and Hathaway announced that he wanted to replace her with Tuesday. "I didn't want her [Novak] for the part anyway. I wanted a younger actress like Tuesday Weld." It seemed like a done deal until the Associated Press carried the story that Novak would be replaced by Tuesday Weld. Kim Novak returned to the set five days later, and it was Henry Hathaway who was replaced by Ken Hughes.

Tuesday acknowledged that her pace was slowing down a bit. "I had a high-stepping, fast-talking life. I shudder when I think of some of the things I did over the past five years. There would be nothing left of me when I reached twenty if I hadn't decided to cut down."

She hinted that she might be contemplating retirement at age twenty-one. "I know I'm not going to spend the rest of my life acting, there's too much else in the world," she said. "I could never be that confined. I think about giving up completely and, not having any money, living on the beach. If you spend your whole life trying to make other people happy, you wind up with nothing. I've got to make myself happy first."

Finally, in late 1964, Tuesday was cast in a motion picture, *The Cincinnati Kid*, for MGM. The film reunited her with Steve McQueen, her co-star from *Soldier in the Rain*. The cast included Edward G. Robinson, Ann-Margret, Karl Malden, Joan Blondell, Rip Torn, and Cab Calloway. Originally, Spencer Tracy was scheduled to play the role of gambler Lancey Howard, but he backed out at the last minute due to ill health and was replaced by Edward G. Robinson.

From the outset, the production was in turmoil. Director Sam Peckinpah was a hard drinker who always seemed to be at war with producers, and this would be no exception. Known for his sudden violent outbursts, Peckinpah sometimes relaxed by throwing knives into doors.

Peckinpah argued constantly with producer Martin Ransohoff over casting. A disagreement occurred over the possible casting of a beautiful young actress named Sharon Tate. Peckinpah had been disappointed with her screen test and had tussled with her. Ransohoff believed that the role would be a great way to launch Sharon Tate's career. Peckinpah won out and Sharon Tate was replaced by Tuesday Weld.

Filming of *The Cincinnati Kid* began on December 1, 1964. Peckinpah spent three days painstakingly shooting a nude scene which would be seen only in European release. Angered over the delays and additional costs, Ransohoff fired Sam Peckinpah. When informed of his dismissal, Peckinpah shouted, "You can take this picture and shove it up your ass!" The studio temporarily shut down production and decided to reshoot the scenes Peckinpah had filmed, taking a half million dollar loss.

Peckinpah's replacement was Canadian-born Norman Jewison. He had come to the United States in the 1950s to direct *Your Hit Parade*, a television program which recapped the week's most popular songs. Jewison became a top television director and won three Emmys before moving into motion pictures. Prior to his work on *The Cincinnati Kid*, Jewison had directed two films starring Doris Day. Jewison was especially skilled with actors and later directed Rod Steiger *(In the Heat of the Night)* and Cher *(Moonstruck)* in their Academy Award-winning performances.

Tuesday Weld's co-star, Ann-Margret, had also been labeled a sex kitten early in her career but, like Tuesday, had developed into a fine actress. She was only nineteen when she was discovered by George Burns in 1960 and experienced one of the fastest rises to stardom of any performer. In one week's time, she was given a screen test by Twentieth Century Fox, signed to a recording contract by RCA, and featured in an article in *Life* magazine. She made her screen debut in *Pocketful of Miracles*, which would be director Frank Capra's last film.

The Cincinnati Kid was based on a best-selling novel by Richard Jessup. Some of the finest screenwriters in Hollywood, including Ring Lardner, Jr., Terry Sothern, and

Paddy Chayefsky, worked on the script. The theme was similar to that of *The Hustler*, except that poker was substituted for pool. It was set in New Orleans during the Depression.

The Cincinnati Kid, Steve McQueen, is an up-and-coming gambler who dreams of challenging Lancey Howard (Edward G. Robinson), the acknowledged king of stud poker. Howard, an aging gambler, knows his days of being on top are numbered, and accepts the Kid's challenge for a winner-take-all game. A former high stakes player, Shooter (Karl Malden), is asked to be the dealer because of his impeccable reputation.

The Kid's backwoods girlfriend, Christian Rudd (Tuesday Weld), arrives in town. While he soaks in a bath tub, Christian describes a foreign film she has just seen. Unlike Shooter, his wife, Melba (Ann-Margret), cheats at everything—including solitaire. She takes the naive Christian on a tour of the wilder side of New Orleans. Christian decides to go back home before the big game. After Christian leaves, Melba seduces The Kid. The showdown comes down to a crucial hand. Everybody thinks The Kid is going to win but incredibly, Howard draws a jack of diamonds for an inside flush which proves to be the winning hand. In shock, The Kid leaves the room to the taunts of Melba and the others.

The European version of the film had a slightly different ending, with The Kid reuniting with Christian. For

Tuesday, the role of the pure Christian was a departure from the bad girl parts she had been playing. She received good reviews for her performance. Howard Thompson of the *The New York Times* wrote: "Tuesday Weld does nicely as his (McQueen's) dimwit sweetie."

The Cincinnati Kid premiered in New Orleans on October 27, 1965. The premiere, which benefitted Hurricane Betsy relief, was ballyhooed as the greatest movie opening in the South since *Gone With the Wind*. The festive atmosphere was shattered when Steve McQueen's mother died of a cerebral hemorrhage on the day of the premiere, and McQueen immediately flew home to California.

Chapter 8

I'll Take Sweden, released in 1965, was a return to light comedy. The film starred Bob Hope, Dina Merrill, and Frankie Avalon. Tuesday Weld was a favorite of Bob Hope and had worked with the comedian on several occasions. She appeared on a television special in 1958, the *Bob Hope Buick Show* in 1961, another Bob Hope special in 1963, and the *Bob Hope Christmas Special* in 1964.

In 1963, Tuesday Weld had accompanied Bob Hope on his Christmas tour of Mediterranean bases. It had become an annual holiday tradition for Bob Hope to entertain American servicemen stationed around the world. Joining Tuesday on the trip were singer Anita Bryant and the reigning Miss U.S.A., Michele Metrinko.

The tour left the United States without Bob Hope, who was recuperating from eye surgery to correct double vision. Comic Jerry Colonna served as the emcee in his absence. For a time there was concern whether Hope would fully regain his vision. On December 22, Hope surprised everyone when he flew to Ankara, Turkey, to join the ensemble. Hope wore specially made black pinhole glasses to protect his eyes.

From Ankara, the tour proceeded to Incirlik, the air base from which Francis Gary Powers had taken off on his infamous U-2 spy flight over Russia. After a stop in Diyarbakir, the tour did a show in Crete, where Anita Bryant collapsed on stage. It was learned that she was pregnant. In Athens, the troupe performed in a giant hangar and were personally welcomed by Prince Constantine and Princess Helen of Greece. The next stop was Wheeler Air Force Base in Tripoli, Libya.

Bob Hope remembered, "Tuesday Weld, surprisingly, turned out to be one of the show's biggest fans. Up till then she'd been one of the top rebels of all time. At first she didn't seem able to relate to any of us. All she wanted to do was perform, run her lines, and give that little prop smile to a lot of people, and then go back and read *Mad* magazine."

Hope assumed Tuesday was up to her old habits when she was fifteen minutes late for the plane leaving Tripoli. Hope was obviously irritated by the delay and demanded to know where she had been. He was surprised when he learned that Tuesday had been at a hospital visiting seriously ill children.

"That was a new kind of Tuesday Weld, a Tuesday Weld who finally got involved," Hope said. Tuesday admitted that she never knew she could care about people that much. The final show of the tour was on the aircraft carrier Shangri-La, anchored off Naples.

Tuesday seemed to be the perfect choice to play Hope's boy-crazy daughter in *I'll Take Sweden*. *I'll Take Sweden* was directed by Fred de Cordova, who had directed Ronald Reagan in *Bedtime for Bonzo*. The slight plot concerned widower Bob Holcomb (Bob Hope) who is troubled by the new, more permissive sexual morality. In particular, he is worried about his daughter, Jo Jo (Tuesday Weld), and her relationship with her motorcycle driving boyfriend, Kenny Klinger (Frankie Avalon). He arranges to be transferred to Sweden for the purpose of separating the young lovers. There, Jo Jo falls for an older playboy (Jeremy Slate) while Bob becomes involved with an attractive interior decorator, Karin Granstedt (Dina Merrill). He realizes that Jo Jo's old boyfriend wasn't so bad after all and flies Kenny to Sweden to break up his daughter's romance with the gigolo.

On July 13, 1965, a month after *I'll Take Sweden* was released, Tuesday Weld again joined Bob Hope on a tour to entertain American servicemen. This time the destination was the Dominican Republic, where 28,000 Marines were stationed by President Johnson to avert a Communist takeover of the country. Bob Hope recalled that Tuesday Weld managed to bring the guerilla war to a temporary halt.

"Naturally Tuesday Weld, the great disappearer, one day found herself on the other side visiting the rebels. It was a strange kind of altercation where you make personal appearances on both sides. Fortunately, both sides knew her, so they called off the war for a few minutes, which, if you've had any experiences with wars, you'll agree is a step in the right direction."

Over the years Tuesday had been romantically involved with a number of men, but she had remained cautious about marriage. "I'd like to get married and have children," she said. "That's the best career move any woman can have, but an actress has to be extremely careful in choosing a man. Actresses usually have lousy husbands—they pick actors—I'd rather not."

Tuesday said that if she did get married it would be to someone who was "creative, intelligent, and witty." Her first husband was not an actor but was involved in the motion picture industry. Claude Harz was a young screenwriter who was working as actor Roddy McDowall's secretary. Tuesday Weld and Claude Harz were married in October, 1965. Roddy McDowall served as the best man at the wedding.

Tuesday felt that the time was right for marriage. "Acting was not fulfilling me, so as rebellious as I always was towards every kind of conditioned thought, I still had the same old ideal dream that marriage and a family was the answer to everything. So I married Claude Harz."

Tuesday's mother didn't approve. She insisted that she wanted what was best for her daughter, but Tuesday believed she had other motives. "Mama hated my husband— she's a jealous lover, you know. She hated all the men I've ever been involved with."

In 1966, Tuesday Weld co-starred with Roddy McDowall in *Lord Love a Duck*. The film was a broad satire of teenage culture in the sixties, its targets ranging from progressive education to beach movies. The supporting cast included Lola Albright, Ruth Gordon, and Harvey Korman.

George Axelrod was making his directorial debut in *Lord Love a Duck*. Axelrod was one of Hollywood's brightest screenwriters. He wrote the screenplays for such box office hits as *The Seven Year Itch*, *Will Success Spoil Rock Hunter*, and *Breakfast at Tiffany's*. The multi-talented Axelrod displayed his versatility as the writer-producer of the dark political thriller, *The Manchurian Candidate*.

In *Lord Love a Duck*, Tuesday plays Barbara Ann Greene, a baton-twirling student at Consolidated High School in Los Angeles. Alan Mugrave (Roddy McDowall), a student with exceptional powers, promises to make all of Barbara Ann's wishes come true. She tells Alan that she wants to be a movie star. "My horoscope tells me I'm going to be famous. I deserve it, too. I've been very good. I haven't done bad things with boys—only if I like the boy."

One of her primary goals is to join an exclusive sorority. The only problem is that each member is required to own at least a dozen cashmere sweaters. Barbara Ann convinces her father to take her shopping. At the store she models sweaters in exotic shades such as papaya surprise, periwinkle pussycat, and pink put-on. Barbara Ann squeals with glee as she rubs the cashmere over her skin. She asks her father, "Don't you love it?" He can barely restrain himself. Barbara Ann lays on her father's lap beneath a pile of sweaters.

Barbara Ann marries Bob Barnard (Martin West), a rich senior majoring in marriage counseling. Everything begins to go wrong for Barbara Ann. Her mother, Marie (Lola Albright), a cocktail waitress, commits suicide because she believes she is an embarrassment to her daughter. Barbara Ann is introduced to a producer of beach movies (his most famous film is *The Thing That Ate Bikini Beach*) and he promises to make her a star. She is devastated when her husband refuses to let her appear in the film.

Alan decides that the only solution is to murder Bob. He tries to kill Bob by poisoning and by tampering with his car but is unsuccessful. On graduation day, Alan accompanies the wheelchair-bound Bob to the ceremonies. He chases him with a bulldozer, finally dispatching him.

Barbara Ann, dressed in a white fur coat, appears at the premiere of her debut film, *Bikini Widow*. Her benefactor, Alan, is confined to a psychiatric ward, where he writes his memoirs.

Lord Love a Duck is funny but uneven. The most controversial scene concerns Barbara Ann's efforts to land a secretarial job in the principal's office. During the interview she sits suggestively on the desk and fondles her breasts. The principal (Harvey Korman) drools as he snaps the pencil he's holding. Needless to say, she gets the job. Perhaps it was this scene he had in mind when critic Rex Reed described the film as pornographic.

George Axelrod had the knack of providing his female stars with their most memorable scenes. In *The Seven Year Itch*, Marilyn Monroe's dress is blown when she stands on a subway grating, revealing her gorgeous legs. The "sweater orgy" scene in *Lord Love a Duck* became Tuesday Weld's most identifiable screen image.

New Yorker film critic Pauline Kael described *Lord Love a Duck as* "the best American comedy of its year, and yet it's mostly terrible." Other critics singled out Tuesday Weld's performance for praise. Judith Crist of the *New York Herald Tribune* wrote: "The best thing about the movie is its display of Tuesday Weld not only as a teenage Lolita of unsurpassed loveliness but also as an actress of unexpected range." Andrew Sarris of the *Village Voice* raved that the cast was "the funniest comic ensemble since the palmiest days of Preston Sturges." Sarris wrote: "Tuesday Weld is Nabokov's grown-up nymphet come to life in a cavalcade of cashmere sweaters and closer to Nabokov's original conception than Sue Lyon could ever be."

Tuesday Weld nearly won the Best Actress Award at the Berlin Film Festival. It was assumed that she was going to win for her performance in *Lord Love a Duck*, and the audience was surprised when it was announced that Lola Albright, who played the supporting role of Tuesday's alcoholic mother, received the award. One of the jurors revealed that the intention was to select Tuesday Weld but that the deciding vote was cast by an unnamed, influential American critic who refused to vote for "that girl." Once again, Tuesday's past reputation had deprived her of the recognition she deserved.

Pauline Kael had her own explanation of why Tuesday Weld had not achieved stardom. "Tuesday Weld has never been one (a star), and maybe it isn't just her unlucky name (If you talk about her ability, people think you're kidding). Maybe it isn't because she hasn't had a big role that would catapult her to fame, either. Maybe it's because she's the kind of actress who doesn't let people know she's acting...How else can one explain an actress giving the performances Tuesday Weld has given in *Rally Round the Flag, Boys!*, *Soldier in the Rain*, *The Cincinnati Kid*, and *Lord Love a Duck* and still not be taken seriously."

Director George Axelrod described *Lord Love a Duck* as a "cross between Andy Hardy and *Dr. Strangelove*." He remarked, "Tuesday Weld is a great natural actress." He marveled at her ability to cry on cue. "She can really cry, not just turn it on."

Tuesday revealed that it was easier to turn on the tears than to turn them off. After a particularly tense day on the set she would cry for hours. "What he [Axelrod] didn't know was the trouble I had turning it off. I cry pretty well. I hold off most emotion until the time comes where it is so built up, I explode, then I cry for a week. When I start crying, you can't stop me."

Tuesday called the experience of working with George Axelrod a "party." She especially enjoyed the freedom he gave his actors. "In kind of a free-form way we did a lot of the work together in writing, a lot of improvisational work." *Lord Love a Duck* became a cult film and one of Tuesday's personal favorites.

She developed a close friendship with her co-star, Roddy McDowall. He said of Tuesday: "She was undervalued year after year. No actress was ever so good in so many bad films." In his book, *Double Exposure*, published in 1966, the year *Lord Love a Duck* was released, McDowall asked Tuesday Weld to profile herself. She wrote an ingenious poem which served as a mini-autobiography. Each line represented a year of her life.

"Tuesday Weld"

1. How would I know?
2. Carried on a lot.
3. Sodas and shoes.
4. Work's a bore.
5. But I'm adored.
6. I can't read.
7. Still can't or even smile.
8. I think I should go away for a while.
9. I retired, quit, for once and for all.
10. I've had my share.
11. When quitting's fair.
12. Tore my mother's hair.
13. Well, I really didn't care.
14. Grown and free, hated everybody.
15. I saw a tree.
16. Tried to kill my mother.
17. Fell in love for one and all.
18. Thought I'd leave him for another.
19. I did.
20. Had a birthday.
21. Now I know real love for once and all.
21 1/2. I painted the tree of memory,
and gave as life, a gift, it away.
22. I saw another tree.

The poem is remarkable in how much it says about Tuesday's life in so few words. It reveals what events were significant to her. She describes her life as a childhood model, her brief retirement, her rebellious stage, conflict with her mother, and broken love affairs. The line which stands out is at age sixteen she tried to kill her mother. When questioned if the line should be taken literally, Tuesday admitted she had used poetic license. "I don't know any sixteen-year-old who doesn't want to kill her mother."

Chapter 9

Pretty Poison

*A*lthough she was not yet twenty-five years old, Tuesday Weld had been in Hollywood for ten years and had appeared in fourteen films. Repeatedly, she had given outstanding performances in less than outstanding films. Fans and critics wondered what she could do if she was ever given a suitable vehicle for her talents.

In 1967, Warren Beatty, the producer and star of *Bonnie and Clyde*, offered Tuesday the plum role of gangster Bonnie Parker. The project originated three years earlier when Robert Benton and David Newman, the art director and editor of *Esquire* magazine, wrote a screenplay based on the lives of bank robbers Bonnie Parker and

Clyde Barrow. They wrote the script with French director Francois Truffaut in mind, but when he turned it down, he referred them to Warren Beatty.

Leslie Caron, Beatty's lover at the time, helped convince him to buy the rights to *Bonnie and Clyde* for ten thousand dollars. None of the major studios were interested in producing the film. When Warner Brothers initially turned him down, Beatty literally got down on his hands and knees and begged. The studio executive motioned for him to get up. "Come on kid, you're embarrassing me," he said. He reluctantly pledged two million dollars for the project.

Leslie Caron had expected to play the role of Bonnie and was devastated when Beatty decided she was not right for the part. He considered a number of actresses including Natalie Wood, Carol Lynley, and even his sister, Shirley MacLaine. Beatty had known Tuesday Weld since their days together on *Dobie Gillis* and thought she was perfect for the part.

Tuesday wanted to do the movie but circumstances prevented her. She was pregnant with her first child, Natasha, during pre-production and once the child was born, she was reluctant to leave her. Beatty had to look elsewhere for his Bonnie. He nearly signed Sue Lyon, the actress who played Lolita, but settled on a then-unknown actress named Faye Dunaway, whom director Arthur Penn had spotted in an Off-Broadway production, *Hogan's Goat*.

Bonnie and Clyde became a landmark film, a critical and commercial hit. Faye Dunaway received an Oscar nomination for best actress and the role made her a star overnight.

One can only imagine how good Tuesday would have been in the part. She had been terrific parodying a gun moll in a dream sequence in *Bachelor Flat*. The role would almost certainly have transformed her into a major star. Many of Tuesday's fans attributed her rejection of the role to a self-destructive nature. Even her mother criticized Tuesday for her poor choice of roles. "You guessed wrong that time, baby, when you turned down *Bonnie and Clyde*," she said.

Tuesday's response was to remind her mother of the questionable judgment she had displayed when she was in control of her career. "After all, she had the wisdom to get me into winners like *Sex Kittens Go to College*. And if I didn't want to do some of the dumb roles she got for me she'd say, 'You owe it to me. Look what I sacrificed for you.'" It took Tuesday years before she was able to tell her mother, "I was the one who sacrificed. I was the kid who stood in front of the camera."

When Tuesday made a bad career decision, she had only herself to blame. "I don't cry so easily nowadays," she said. "That's because I make the decisions that affect me instead of letting Mama do it."

Besides, she was preoccupied with being a wife and mother. During her pregnancy she stopped drinking, fearing that it might affect her unborn child. Over the years, Tuesday had tried various forms of therapy including psychoanalysis, psychotherapy, and hypnosis. A friend, writer-director Tom Mankiewicz, referred her to Dr. Frederick Hacker, one of Hollywood's best-known analysts. Hacker had established the first comprehensive psychiatric clinic in Los Angeles and his clients included Robert Mitchum.

"I went into analysis for a year when I couldn't cope with anything anymore, and my shrink taught me how to be self-indulgent. If your thing is to be a doughnut, go ahead and dip into the chocolate sauce and be a great doughnut."

Tuesday was more concerned with being a great mother than a great doughnut. She was determined that Natasha would not have to face the pressures she had encountered as a child. She vowed to keep her hands off her daughter's life and let her make her own decisions whenever possible. Asked if she would encourage Natasha to become an actress, Tuesday exclaimed, "No way! I'm not going to even allow her near a sound stage."

She considered retiring from acting to become a full-time wife and mother. "I felt what I had been doing up to that time was probably wrong, and I should be a housewife." But Tuesday soon found the role of being a housewife unfulfilling. "For a while it was great, but then it started to drive me nuts," she said. "The amount of energy it takes for me to make a bed or do the dishes sends me into deep depression."

After much contemplation, Tuesday decided she could still be a good wife and mother without sacrificing her acting career. In May, 1967, she played Abigail in a celebrated CBS presentation of Arthur Miller's *The Crucible*. The David Susskind production also starred George C. Scott, Colleen Dewhurst, and Fritz Weaver.

Unexpectedly, at this crucial moment in her career, Tuesday was offered what many fans and critics regard as her best role. At first glance, *Pretty Poison* had little to distinguish it. The director, Noel Black, was a thirty-year-old graduate of the UCLA Film School who had limited experience as a television director. *Pretty Poison* marked his feature film debut.

The story was based on a little-known novel, *She Let Him Continue*, by Stephen Geller. The screenwriter, Lorenzo Semple, Jr., was best known as a script consultant for the *Batman* television series. He later wrote the screenplays for the political thrillers *Three Days of the Condor* and *The Parallax View*.

Tuesday's co-star, Anthony Perkins, was the son of a noted actor of the 1920s, Osgood Perkins. He had known Tuesday for a number of years and described her as "very hip." Perkins received an Oscar nomination in 1956 for his performance as a Quaker in *Friendly Persuasion*. Four years later, he starred as the demented Norman Bates in Alfred

Hitchcock's *Psycho*. Perkins was so convincing in the role that it typecast him for the rest of his career.

Pretty Poison takes place in a small Massachusetts industrial town. Dennis Pitt (Anthony Perkins) has been released from an institution where he has been confined since he burned down his aunt's house as a youth. On being released, he gets a job at the Sausenfeld Chemical Plant. One day he watches a high school drill team practice. Carrying the flag is an attractive blonde, Sue Ann Stepanek (Tuesday Weld).

He meets Sue Ann at Pete's Diner where he piques her interest by posing as a CIA agent. He suggests that she might be of assistance in his top-secret mission. Dennis tells Sue Ann that a subversive group is poisoning the local water supply.

Dennis gets fired when the owner of the chemical plant learns he is a convicted arsonist. He informs Sue Ann that it is necessary to make a night raid to sabotage the chemical plant. Sue Ann introduces Dennis to her mother (Beverly Garland). She tries to pass Dennis off as a friend of the family, but Mrs. Stepanek catches her in the lie. She slaps Sue Ann, who slaps her back even harder.

After dark, Dennis and Sue Ann go to the chemical plant. Dennis' plan is to loosen the chute which pours pollution into the river. He figures that the structure will collapse with the first load in the morning. A night watchman confronts Dennis. Sue Ann strikes the watchman on the back of the head with a wrench, knocking him unconscious. Sue Ann gleefully reports to Dennis, "I hit him twice." She looks at the fallen watchman and matter-of-factly says, "He sure is bleeding, isn't he?"

She straddles the night watchman and pushes his face beneath the water. She has a simulated orgasm as the man drowns. Sue Ann places the body right under the chute so when it collapses it will appear that the death was accidental. "God, what a night!" Sue Ann remarks with a smile on her face. The violence has excited her and she wants to make love to Dennis.

They drive to a Lovers' Lane where they are interrupted by two policemen, who are unaware of the murder. They take Dennis and Sue Ann to her mother's house. When the police leave, Mrs. Stepanek warns Dennis never to see Sue Ann again.

The next morning the chute collapses just as Dennis and Sue Ann planned. Sue Ann suggests that they run away together and get married. Sue Ann and Dennis return to her house to pack while her mother is away. When Mrs. Stepanek arrives home unexpectedly, Sue Ann orders Dennis to shoot her. Dennis refuses and Sue Ann grabs the gun and shoots her mother as she comes up the steps. She licks her lips as she pulls the trigger. Dennis throws up in the bathroom while Sue Ann lies on the bed and giggles.

Now totally in control, Sue Ann instructs Dennis to throw her mother's body in the trunk and dump it into the lake. Dennis, overwhelmed by the murder, decides to turn himself over to the police. When he enters the police station he sees Sue Ann tearfully telling the police that Dennis had murdered her mother right before her eyes. As the police drag Dennis away, Sue Ann swigs on a Pepsi. She laments, "I feel a little bit responsible for mom's death myself."

Unlike their combative relationship in the film, Tuesday Weld and Beverly Garland enjoyed a positive relationship off screen. "She was wonderful in that picture. We became friends—easy and kind with each other. Two women who respected each other and gave to each other their best. What a delight she was."

Tuesday Weld's chilling portrayal of Sue Ann Stepanek, the all-American girl turned murderess, was the most memorable of her career. The character is a combination of Thalia Menninger and the blind murderess she played on *The Fugitive*. For Sue Ann violence is an aphrodisiac. She subtly takes control of Dennis, using him to get rid of her mother. The pretty poison being dumped in the river is not nearly as deadly as the pretty poison in the high school majorette's outfit.

Critical response to Tuesday's performance was unanimous. Rex Reed wrote that *Pretty Poison* "reestablished her as a major talent." *Time* magazine wrote: "She mixes innocence with evil to chilling effect, etching her character with acid and honey." Even John Simon, generally the most acerbic of critics, praised the film: "Rush to see *Pretty Poison*; it has the taste of bitter truth, which once again is proving poison at the box office."

Pauline Kael, film critic of the *New Yorker*, also urged her readers to hurry to see the film. "When I discovered that *Pretty Poison* had opened without advance publicity or screenings, I rushed to see it, because a movie that makes the movie companies so nervous they're afraid to show it to the critics stands an awfully good chance of being an interesting movie. This is a remarkable first feature film by a gifted young American, Noel Black."

About the only person who didn't like the film was Tuesday Weld. She called it her least favorite film. She believed her performance was a rehashing of old material.

"I don't care if the critics like it; I hated it," Tuesday insisted. "I can't be objective about films I had a terrible time doing."

Tuesday enjoyed working with the cast but fought continually with Noel Black, whose approach to moviemaking was not to her liking. She always preferred assertive direction. "My major fault is that I've never had enough discipline," Tuesday admitted. "I need a strong director who knows how to handle me and can. Otherwise, I lose respect and interest."

She described her method of motivation. "I have to make myself excited by the dialogue of the character or something in a scene. Sometimes a director will say, 'Do whatever you like,' and that makes it difficult."

Tuesday calls *Pretty Poison* "the least creative experience I ever had." Her memories of the picture are almost all negative. "Constant hate, turmoil, and dissonance. Not a day went by without a fight. Noel Black, the director, would come up to me before a scene and say, 'Think about Coca Cola.' I finally said, 'Look, just give the directions to Tony Perkins and he'll interpret them for me.'"

She contemptuously stated, "I learned more from the old *Dobie Gillis* shows on TV than from *Pretty Poison*." Tuesday was probably right when she said, "If it hadn't been for the fuss the critics raised about *Pretty Poison*, I'll bet it wouldn't have gotten wide release."

Twentieth Century Fox tried to release the film in March, 1968, but couldn't find a distributor. Exhibitors argued that a film starring Anthony Perkins and Tuesday Weld couldn't be taken seriously. When *Pretty Poison* previewed in Los Angeles, it bombed. At one screening, not a single reviewer showed up. Neither Tuesday Weld nor Anthony Perkins believed enough in the film to actively promote it.

When *Pretty Poison* was officially released in New York on October 23, 1968, the timing couldn't have been worse. The year 1968 had seen the assassinations of the Reverend Martin Luther King, Jr., and Robert Kennedy as well as the escalation of the Vietnam War. The country was not in the mood for a dark, violent film. *Pretty Poison*, despite its rave reviews, proved to be a box office failure.

Despite the film's limited release, Tuesday Weld was voted runner-up (behind Joanne Woodward) for best actress by the New York Film Critics. She finished ahead of an elite roster of actresses including Katharine Hepburn, Patricia Neal, and Barbra Streisand. Author Danny Peary in his book, *Alternative Oscars*, argues that Tuesday Weld deserved to win the Oscar that year instead of the co-recipients, Katharine Hepburn and Barbra Streisand. At the time, however, it was unthinkable for the Academy to nominate Tuesday Weld for best actress, especially for a small film which died at the box office.

Tuesday was no longer ignored by Hollywood producers. She was offered roles in major Hollywood productions but inevitably she turned them down. She turned down a starring role (eventually played by Kim Darby) opposite John Wayne in *True Grit*. The film was a hit and earned Wayne his only Academy Award. She also passed on *Bob & Carol & Ted & Alice*, another box office smash. The part resulted in an Oscar nomination for Dyan Cannon and made her a star. Tuesday also rejected the role in *Cactus Flower* for which Goldie Hawn won her Oscar for Best Supporting Actress in 1969.

Tuesday says she has no regrets about turning down the coveted roles. She proclaimed, "I do not ever want to be a huge star." She explained: "Do you think I want a success? I refused *Bonnie and Clyde* because I was nursing at the time but also because deep down I knew that it was going to be a huge success. The same was true of *Bob and Carol and Fred and Sue* or whatever it was called. It reeked of success."

Actor Ryan O'Neal expressed his admiration for her attitude. "She's held in very high esteem because she's a survivor and because she's good. She's like a war hero, and she deserves the Congressional Medal. The only thing that bothers her is—what else?—success."

Another film which would have insured her stardom was *Rosemary's Baby*. Based on the best-selling novel by Ira Levin, it's the story of a woman who gives birth to the devil's child. The film was to be directed by the Polish director Roman Polanski. Tuesday Weld was his first choice for the lead because he admired her work and because she was a friend of his wife, Sharon Tate. Paramount insisted on a star with more box office clout and selected Mia Farrow. A few years later, Polanski wanted Tuesday Weld to star in his film version of *Macbeth*. She lost the part when she refused to do a nude sleepwalking scene. The role was eventually played by Francesca Annis.

Tuesday took the disappointments in stride. "If I found myself in a commercial success, I'd probably go into a state of shock. If I get out of this underground thing and become commercial, I don't know what I'll do."

Chapter 10

I Walk the Line

Tuesday's first film of the seventies was *I Walk the Line* for Columbia Pictures. Her co-stars were two Oscar winners, Gregory Peck and Estelle Parsons. The director, John Frankenheimer, had a string of hits to his credit including *Birdman of Alcatraz*, *The Manchurian Candidate*, *Seven Days in May*, and *Grand Prix*.

The title for the film was taken from the Johnny Cash country classic. Cash sang five songs on the soundtrack. The movie opens with a pickup truck speeding down a country road. Inside the truck are Alma McCain (Tuesday Weld) and her young brother, Buddy. The local sheriff, Henry Tawes (Gregory Peck), pulls over the truck. Buddy runs away, leaving Alma to face the sheriff. The older man is immediately attracted to the country girl with the corn-silk colored hair. She persuades him to let her go free with just a warning.

Alma returns home to her moonshiner father, Carl (Ralph Meeker). He asks Alma if she thinks Sheriff Tawes is suspicious of their moonshining. Despite being married, the sheriff has an affair with young Alma. He discovers the McCain still but overlooks it because of his infatuation with Alma.

Tawes' wife, Ellen (Estelle Parsons), suspects that he's having an affair. He decides to ask Alma to run off with him to California. He doesn't know that she's already married and her husband is in prison. The sheriff's deputy, Hunnicut (Charles Durning), finds the still and infers to Alma that he's willing to look the other way if she has sex with him. Alma's father returns and kills the deputy.

Sheriff Tawes arrives as the family is burying Hunnicutt in a shallow grave. He is shocked by the murder but promises he will let the rest of the family escape if they leave Alma with him. After the sheriff helps conceal the grave, he discovers the McCain family, including Alma, are gone. Tawes tracks them in his police car until he corners them on an isolated country road. Alma huddles in the back of the pickup truck with her little brother. She refuses to leave her family. When the sheriff shoots her father during a scuffle, Alma stabs him in the arm with a meat hook. The McCains drive away, leaving the sheriff wounded by the roadside facing a shattered marriage and career.

Tuesday enjoyed working with director John Frankenheimer whom she described as "wonderful." Co-star Gregory Peck was less pleased with how the film turned out. He recalled, "My whole preoccupation was with the meaning and style of the picture. I knew that it was not coming off.

"The picture lost its meaning for me when the prologue and epilogue were eliminated. When Johnny Cash's songs were tacked on, with the lyrics explaining everything that was happening on the screen, as though the audience couldn't comprehend it on their own. I knew it was a lost cause. Frankenheimer said to me later, 'Greg, I owe you one.'"

Although Peck was disappointed with the film, he found no fault with Tuesday Weld's performance. "Tuesday is an original and effective actress. Everyone agrees on that. She was there to play a role, and did it perfectly in her own unique way."

Tuesday also respected Peck as an actor but recalled they did not approach an intimate love scene in the same manner. "We had to do a love scene in bed and it showed my bare back. I wasn't nude or anything, maybe a half slip, I don't remember exactly, but I was as nude as possible. And he [Peck] got into bed with his pants and his shoes on.

Now they weren't moccasins. They were big clunky busi-
nessman's shoes, laced up. With socks on...What more
can I say?"

Gregory Peck's personal modesty resulted in the alter-
ation of another scene. Peck was supposed to swim under-
water through the flooded rooms of his childhood home on
land which had been taken over by the Tennessee Valley
Authority. Director Frankenheimer wanted Peck to do the
scene in the nude, promising to shoot only from the rear.
Peck objected, stating, "I'll wear a diving suit. I make my
living with my brains, not my behind."As a result, the scene
was cut from the movie.

Tuesday's performance as a teenage mountain girl was
convincing. Danny Kaye had once said Tuesday was "fifteen going on twenty-seven." Now it could be said she
was twenty-seven going on fifteen.Tuesday received good
notices. *Variety* reported: "Miss Weld is striking as the
moonshiner's daughter, capturing just the right accent
and qualities of late teenage sensuality, amorality, and
dumb innocence to make her a fatal attraction for an
older married man."

Howard Thompson, the film critic of *The New York
Times*, singled out Tuesday's performance for praise: "The
exception is Tuesday Weld, whose performance as a childlike but worldly country girl is as natural and picturesque
as the backgrounds."

I Walk the Line opened in New York on November 18, 1970. The downbeat theme and the country setting did not appeal to urban audiences. *The New York Times* noted that the film opened one week and closed the next. A few weeks later, Eugene Archer of the *Times* wrote of Tuesday: "It's no secret that she's good, very, very good, and sometimes a little better than that. Why is such a gifted actress still not a star?"

With her professional career at a standstill, Tuesday's five-year marriage to Claude Harz was on the rocks. Tuesday explained that her notoriety was a contributing factor to their marital problems. "The marriage was disastrous. It was my house, my friends, my position, my world, but nothing happened to him. I felt so guilty, I smoked three packs of cigarettes a day, took pills, and drank so steadily for ten years that people who know me well don't know how I came out of it alive. I would drink anything, everything, it didn't matter. I drank morning, noon, and night."

The prospects of appearing on a television talk show became a traumatic experience. Tuesday recalled, "I thought [if] I could first go on Dick Cavett without having to get drunk first, I could get through anything. I locked myself in my hotel room for two days and wouldn't talk to anyone. I wouldn't even let them interview me ahead of time. I just wanted to walk on the show cold and let it all come out."

Tuesday's marriage to Claude Harz ended in divorce. "I didn't ask Claude for alimony," Tuesday said. "Part of my reason was liberation. I'm all for women's lib. But it's men's liberation as much as women's. I don't see any reason for Claude to have that obligation hanging over his head. I don't expect anything from him. He's young and just getting started. If he has the money, I'm sure he'll give it to me."

When asked further about her views on women's lib, Tuesday replied, "Women's lib? I'm in and out. I don't like groups. I represent me."

Tuesday considered the marriage a mistake. "It seems the brighter you are, the deeper the hole you fall into. How can people endure pain for so long and continue to stay together?" When asked if she would marry again, she sounded a little like Thalia Menninger. "Marriage? I'm soured on the idea. If I every marry again, it would be for money. I mean enough money so I never have to worry about providing for somebody else; I've always supported everybody. It's time someone supported me."

The one good thing which came out of the marriage was her daughter, Natasha. Tuesday declared, "I'm more proud of her than anything else in the world." When Natasha was two-and-a-half, Tuesday took her to live in London for a year. "I didn't want to inflict any more pain on myself," Tuesday remembered. "I didn't know anyone there…I just wanted to be totally anonymous and somehow I was able to pull myself out of my deep depression."

Just as Tuesday appeared to be recovering, the unthinkable happened. Tuesday had flown to Catalina when she learned that her house had burned down. At the time her daughter and housekeeper were at home. Frantically, she tried to charter a boat to take her back to the mainland but high winds delayed her turn. The telephone lines were down, so she couldn't even telephone to check on the safety of her daughter. After four hours of this hell of uncertainty, she was finally able to return home. She described the scene: "When I finally did get back, where my house had been was just about four or five piles of ashes. And I was walking through it thinking, 'Am I walking through my daughter?'"

It seemed like an eternity before Tuesday learned that the housekeeper had taken Natasha to her house in Santa Monica. It was a close call. The housekeeper was about to take a shower when she decided to check on Natasha and saw there were flames all around the room. She grabbed the child and ran from the burning building. Much of the housekeeper's hair had been burned off.

Tuesday's relief upon learning that her daughter was safe more than compensated for the loss of her possessions. "Later I went to look at the ashes but I didn't cry. I had been through this before when another house of mine was washed way in a flood. Aside from five years of journals I was keeping for a book and fifteen paintings, none of it mattered." Still, the loss was considerable, both financially and personally. She had carefully selected her possessions to represent herself. "Suddenly, I felt naked," she admitted.

Tuesday's reaction was to move further to detach herself from material things. She realized that her identity wasn't based on her possessions, but on her inner self. "This is me," she said. "It's all inside."

The last link to past possessions was destroyed when she reported, "My 1962 Porsche broke down and will never work again. All my roots exploded at once."

She confided to interviewer Rex Reed, "I know something's wrong. I'm a displaced person. I really feel like I'm starting everything all over again."

Restless, she would walk the streets at night, sometimes several miles at a time. The one possession she still treasured was the most precious—her daughter Natasha. When they traveled, their material possessions filled one suitcase apiece. Tuesday expressed the uncertainty of her existence. "I have no pets, just Tasha. She's my only pet. And I will never own anything again. I don't know where I want to live, who I want to be, or what I want to do."

In a span of a year, Tuesday Weld had endured a lifetime's share of misfortune what with her divorce and the loss of all her possessions. As the shock wore off, a feeling of catharsis emerged as she began to rise from the ashes. "Half of me feels so incredibly old and tired, and the other half hasn't even begun, hasn't touched the good, whole part of life. That's why I'm wandering around. I'm suspended, floating. I'm not happy, and I'm not sad. But, for the first time, I feel really free. Free from my husband. Free from my mother."

Incredibly Tuesday came to regard this time of adversity as a positive experience. "This is the first year I've ever been happy," she said. Years before she had confessed, "I am a defeatist. I thrive on misery…I must have misery. That's been true ever since I was born."

One of the things which helped her keep her balance was her writing. She kept journals, wrote poetry, and even considered writing a screenplay. Tuesday started to write a novel which contained autobiographical material. "It's going to be a good book," she promised. "But I may have to wait until my ex-husband and mother die before I publish it."

She began to put her life in perspective. "I know I'll get it all together in my own way. I really feel like I'm starting everything over again. I know now it's not important to be happy all the time, as long as I keep moving, progressing. This trouble is the best way for me to come out of my shell."

For the first time in ten years, Tuesday began to grant interviews. Previously, she considered interviews an invasion of her privacy but now she recognized their therapeutic value. She observed, "It's almost like going to an analyst—and there's no fee."

Tuesday discovered that many people cared for her and, despite (or maybe because of) her lack of success at the box office, she had a large and devoted following. The strength of the Tuesday Weld cult became apparent in 1971, when a Tuesday Weld Film Festival was held at the Eighth Street Playhouse in New York City. It was the most publicized of the many Tuesday Weld festivals which were staged around the country over the years. At first, Tuesday was skeptical that such a cult existed.

"People tell me there's a Tuesday Weld cult but producers tell me my films don't make money. They just gather good reviews and lose money."

She didn't know how to react to her cult status. "The first festival made me feel a little strange, because they usually give the festivals for Greta Garbo or someone who's older or dead. I was in my early twenties, and they were showing something like ten films. I didn't even know what it meant. I didn't go to the festival. The only one I ever went to was in San Francisco; and I still didn't have any idea what that was all about."

Eventually, she enjoyed her cult status. "I may be self-destructive, but I like taking chances with movies. I like challenges and I also like the particular position I've been in all these years, with people wanting to save me from all the awful films I've been in. I'm happy being a legend. I think the Tuesday Weld cult is a very nice thing."

Tuesday confirmed her reputation as a survivor, realizing that the adversity had only made her stronger. "So many unfortunate things have happened to me in the last few years, but I've been able to survive them all without cracking up. Now I can survive anything."

"It's been a pattern in my life that when something has been completed, it has always meant disaster of some kind," she said. "When I had my car redone, it was stolen. When I had my house just the way I wanted it, it burned down...If something is not completed, it means life is going on and you still have something more to do, but God forbid that you have it all finished and fixed and set—death!"

On the other hand, Tuesday felt she was overdue for some good luck. "Maybe it's time for my renaissance," she mused.

Chapter 11

A Safe Place

A Safe Place was Tuesday Weld's most experimental and controversial film. Henry Jaglom, now considered one of America's leading directors of independent films, was making his directorial debut. Jaglom's breakthrough came as the result of his masterful editing of *Easy Rider*. The overwhelming success of that landmark film provided Jaglom with the opportunity to direct.

Jaglom's biggest coup was to convince major stars such as Tuesday Weld, Jack Nicholson, and Orson Welles to appear in a first film with an extremely limited budget. Henry Jaglom had known Tuesday since the days he was a young actor in New York in the early 1960s. When he came to California in 1965, he lived with Tuesday for six months. He was amazed by her maturity. "She was more completely herself at age 20 than anyone I've seen."

Over the years the two young actors spent a great deal of time together. Jaglom recalled appearing on stage with Tuesday at a Sunset Strip nightclub, pretending to be hypnotized by Pat Collins, a performer known as the "Hip Hypnotist." On another occasion, they shared a limousine with the Beatles on one of their American tours.

On November 22, 1963, Tuesday and Henry were planning to go out to dinner when they heard the news of the Kennedy assassination. Formally dressed, they spent the day at producer Dan Melnick's home, somberly watching the news coverage of the tragedy.

Jack Nicholson's rise to the top in Hollywood had been a slow one. He began his show business career inauspiciously, earning $30 a week sorting fan mail at MGM for the cartoon characters Tom and Jerry. Nicholson failed his first screen test when he froze and forgot his lines. Throughout the sixties, he appeared in a number of low-budget horror and biker movies. His big break occurred in 1969, at age 32 when he received an Oscar nomination for his performance as the renegade lawyer in *Easy Rider*. Actually, Nicholson almost turned down the part because he was required to cut his hair.

After starring roles in *Five Easy Pieces* and *Carnal Knowledge*, Jack Nicholson was commanding a six-figure salary, far more than Henry Jaglom could afford. They had known each other since their days together at the West Coast Actors Studio. When Nicholson directed his first film, *Drive, He Said*, Jaglom appeared in it as an actor. Now Nicholson returned the favor, agreeing to star in Jaglom's first film, *A Safe Place*. Nicholson told Jaglom he needed a new color television set and that he would waive his large salary if he would buy him one.

The task of convincing Orson Welles to star in the movie was a greater challenge. Welles had stunned Hollywood in 1941, when he directed, produced, co-authored, and starred in *Citizen Kane*, a film widely regarded by many now as the greatest film of all time. At age 25, his future seemed unlimited. But Welles was never again given the creative control he had for *Citizen Kane*, and his career was reduced to occasional acting and directing assignments. Hollywood's *enfant terrible* had become a victim of the American youth culture. Welles lamented, "America treated me like a god. If you're only young enough in America you can demand the world and they'll give it to you. Now I'm over 40, so America lost interest in me."

Henry Jaglom revered Welles but had never met him. Another director, Peter Bogdanovich, arranged for a meeting between the two men. Jaglom flew to New York, where he went to Welles' suite at the Plaza Hotel. Welles, wearing blue silk pajamas, opened the door.

"Oh, it's you," he said gruffly. "You've got five minutes."

When Jaglom explained that he wasn't sure what role he had in mind for him Welles exclaimed, "Get the fuck out of here!" Jaglom begged for one more chance. He quickly improvised, remembering that Welles was a magic buff. He promised Welles that he could play a magician.

"Can I wear a cape?" Welles asked.

The cape was the selling point, and Welles agreed to appear in the film. Once on the set, Jaglom may have regretted that he had been so persuasive. Welles tried to take charge of the film, instructing Tuesday Weld and even Jaglom as if he were the director. As much as he admired Welles, Jaglom realized that he needed to retake control of the situation. Jaglom liked to do scenes in one take and Welles preferred multiple takes. Jaglom offered Welles a compromise: he could do as many takes as he wanted if he would stop trying to direct. The arrangement worked perfectly and Welles never gave him any more trouble.

Tuesday got along very well with Orson. According to Henry Jaglom, Welles was fascinated by her.

Jaglom's directing methods were unconventional to say the least. He gave his actors an outline; however, ninety percent of the dialogue was improvised. He insisted on working with actors who he knew were emotionally complex. He simply let the actors be themselves, writing the script to conform to their personalities.

Jaglom was convinced that Jack Nicholson was an old-fashioned star in a league with Humphrey Bogart and Clark

Gable. He felt Nicholson could carry a picture on the strength of his personality. He didn't specify what Nicholson's role entailed except that he was the hero. In his words, "He would fuck the girl, fuck the audience, fuck the movie; save the girl, save the audience, save the movie."

Jaglom also had some unusual ideas about the interaction between actors. The director kept Tuesday and Jack Nicholson apart as long as possible. Nicholson had never met Tuesday Weld. Years before, when he was an unknown, he had seen her in nightspots around Hollywood. Now, both stars were eager to meet each other. Jaglom intentionally didn't introduce them until just before an important love scene. The strategy worked, and the chemistry between Weld and Nicholson was electric.

Jaglom had conceived the idea for *A Safe Place* when he was studying at the Actors' Studio in the early sixties. He based the main character, whom he named Noonie, on Tuesday. The idea was well received by his fellow actors and he was determined to make it into a movie once he had the opportunity. When he was given the chance to direct his own film after the success of *Easy Rider*, *A Safe Place* was his first choice.

In the film, a young woman named Noah (Tuesday Weld) lives alone in New York. She is a disturbed flower child, who retreats into her past, yearning for lost innocence. She recalls her childhood, searching for a "safe place." As a child she met a magician (Orson Welles) in

Central Park who presented her with magical objects: a levitating silver ball, a star ring, and a Noah's ark.

Noah lives in her own world, a world in which she can never grow up. She is romantically involved with two totally different men. Fred (Philip Proctor) is practical but dull. Mitch (Jack Nicholson) is dynamic and sexy, her ideal fantasy partner. Neither man is able to totally fulfill her needs. Fred discovers her body in the bathtub, an apparent suicide.

Despite co-starring with two major stars in Hollywood, Jack Nicholson and Orson Welles, Tuesday Weld received top billing. The film was a showcase for Tuesday. In one of her most memorable scenes, she has a fantasy about the sexual properties of telephone numbers. She nearly goes into ecstasy thinking about prefixes such as Plaza and Gramercy. "It's all on the dial," she explains. It was a scene only Tuesday could have pulled off. It was her most personal role. Henry Jaglom said, "Tuesday Weld's never been more who she is than in *A Safe Place*. It is, I think, Tuesday's quintessential performance, using more of her and more deeply than any other time."

Jaglom acknowledged that Tuesday was a major influence. "She changed the whole way I did films," he admitted. "She taught me to be true to myself." At first, he tried giving conventional direction to Tuesday. He soon realized that she was more interesting than the scene he proposed.

As a result, he gave his actors the freedom to be themselves and improvise.

He was gratified by the richness and depth of her performance. "Tuesday was incredibly great to work with," he recalled. "She was fresh, spontaneous, open. She gave emotionally more than anyone."

Tuesday identified completely with the character. "The part was written for me and about me. I'm really that girl, Noah, except that I don't want to go anywhere near my past. I would like to develop amnesia about it."

Henry Jaglom described his film as "an essay on time and memory." He had no idea how his unconventional film would be received by studio executives. According to Jaglom, Leo Jaffe, an executive at Columbia, told him, "Jesus, I didn't even piss once during the screening." He explained that he normally went to the bathroom at least a dozen times during the screening of a film because they rarely held his interest. He told Jaglom that *A Safe Place* was so different that he couldn't take his eyes off the screen.

Jaglom was astonished when Columbia attempted to market *A Safe Place* as a conventional love story. The studio had just scored a major box office hit with *Love Story* and hoped a similar publicity campaign might attract an audience.

Tuesday Weld was cautiously optimistic about the film's chances. "But if you're not exactly a box office panic, at least you don't have to top your last success. That could work for me on *A Safe Place*. I hope so. I want that to be a success for Henry. He's a personal friend of mine."

A Safe Place was screened at the 1971 New York Film Festival. The film received a mixed reaction: a mixture of loud boos and scattered, fervent applause. In the audience, Tuesday Weld was annoyed by the response, in particular one extremely vocal critic. When Tuesday tried to defend the film the man shouted, "Shut up, Tuesday! You're pretty but you're stupid." Tuesday responded by throwing something at the heckler and pandemonium broke loose.

Everyone's fears were realized when the film bombed at the box office. It was too far out of the mainstream to attract a large audience, even with its remarkable cast. It was the kind of film you either loved or hated. Some critics found the film confusing and self-indulgent. Others praised it as being innovative, thought-provoking, and magical. Critic Maurice Peterson wrote: "It is definitely one of the most exciting experiments in cinema of this, or any year." The *Free Press* ran three separate reviews of *A Safe Place*, praising it as "an important milestone in the art form of the motion picture." Jaglom's most enthusiastic supporter was the celebrated author Anais Nin. She called the film a masterpiece and compared Jaglom to the great Italian director Federico Fellini. Nin was so impressed that she offered to sell the American rights of all her books to Henry Jaglom for one dollar.

Tuesday Weld received some of her most glowing reviews of her career for *A Safe Place*. Vincent Canby of *The New York Times* wrote: "Miss Weld, a lovely young woman with large sad eyes and a few barely discernible freckles, is enchanting to watch—a mysterious mixture of childlike grace and aggressive eroticism." Another critic, Douglas Broade, observed: "For the female lead Jaglom chose Tuesday Weld, an actress as brilliant as she is beautiful, though a woman of dubious taste in film projects and an apparent death wish so far as her career is concerned." Maurice Peterson perhaps best capsulized Tuesday Weld's mystique: "She may well be the most mysteriously appealing star of our day. She is at a glance a vamp; at an angle a little girl; in closeup a jewel—perfect beauty with a marble surface and fiery core."

Despite their failures at the box office, Tuesday rated *A Safe Place* and *Lord Love a Duck* as her favorite films because they represent "my mistakes, me. I don't care if anybody else likes them."

Although critics were generally kind to her, Tuesday was never swayed by their opinions. "I only read good reviews. I'm too easily influenced by negative things. If I'm with a bunch of dopers, I'll follow them right to the opium den. So I never read negative reviews. I had enough of defending the name Tuesday Weld as a child. They can't hurt me now. I've outgrown that insecurity. I've outgrown the jokes about my name. Critics can't change or rectify anything. All you can learn from them is a few words. I select all my movies out of instinct, not because of what critics will think."

After her house burned down, Tuesday led a nomadic existence. "I feel misplaced everywhere," she said. For a time, she lived in a small suite in an out-of-the-way New York hotel. Her accommodations were definitely unstar-like. The door was propped open with a cardboard Sylvania light bulb box. Tuesday was always locking herself out of her apartment, and it was a common sight to see her walking barefoot to the front desk to ask for a spare key. The ash-trays were filled with unsmoked cigarettes. "I never smoke them," she explained. "I just hold them in my mouth."

Tuesday discovered a new way of meeting people. Like almost everything else she did, it was unconventional. "The important thing now is my friends. I spend a lot of time hitchhiking. As a consequence, I find my friends are now people who don't own anything. They're not in show business and they all hate each other. So I'm lucky. I can have five different kinds of evenings in one week."

Tuesday attempted a reconciliation with her mother. "We fought a great deal over the years but I said to myself, 'I'm older now and Mama's a grandmother.'" She hoped that Natasha might bring them closer together, but the re-sentment was still too great. "It was impossible," Tuesday sighed. "To this day, Mama thinks I owe everything to her."

After her divorce, Tuesday began dating other men. She admitted, "I adore men, I like being around them, and I fall in love a lot."

One of her dates was comedian David Steinberg. His sharp-edged humor contributed to the cancellation of the *Smothers Brothers Comedy Hour*. The show had been under fire from CBS censors for its controversial stand on censorship and its opposition to the Vietnam War. Steinberg guest-starred on the program, reading a comic sermonette which was to be aired on Easter. CBS objected to a portion of the sermon which referred to the story of Jonah and the whale. When the Smothers Brothers refused to edit out the offensive reference, their show was cancelled.

In her late twenties, Tuesday Weld underwent a transformation, both physically and as an actress. The prettiness of her teenage years had blossomed into a delicate beauty. As an actress her depth and range had grown enormously and she looked for parts which reflected her maturity. One role which appealed to her was the disturbed actress in *Play It As It Lays*.

"Frank Perry is trying to talk me into doing *Play It As It Lays*. I could do that neurotic girl, alienated in the Hollywood snake pit. I've been there. But I can take it or leave it. The secret is not success, but knowing when to get out. I do not plan to be an actress the rest of my life or do a bad TV series when I'm thirty-five just because I'm restless for the camera. By that time I'll be out of the business and doing something else."

Director Frank Perry insisted that Tuesday Weld was the only actress who could play the part. "She knows the role so well she could phone it in. I tested hundreds of girls for the part, but I always knew it had to be Tuesday."

Perry's persistence paid off and Tuesday agreed to star in the film for Universal. Like Jaglom's, Perry's films were unconventional, highly personal and thought-provoking. His best-known films, *David and Lisa*, *The Swimmer*, and *Last Summer*, had devoted cult followings. Actually, Sam Peckinpah had been the original choice as the director for *Play It As It Lays* but was replaced by Frank Perry before shooting began. It marked the third time that Tuesday Weld had narrowly missed working with the controversial director.

Tuesday was again teamed with Anthony Perkins. They performed brilliantly together in *Pretty Poison* and had a mutual respect. Perkins said of Tuesday, "She's one of the last independent minded actresses of her generation. She's great." Weld described Perkins as simply "the best."

Based on the Joan Didion novel, *Play It As It Lays* targets the emptiness of the Hollywood lifestyle. Tuesday Weld plays Maria Wyeth, an ex-model and B-movie actress. She strolls the grounds of a mental hospital, recalling the traumatic events which led to her breakdown. She is married to an unfaithful, self-engrossed director, Carter Lane

(Adam Roarke). Neglected by her husband, Maria engages in a series of one-night stands and becomes pregnant. Her husband divorces her, and she has an illegal abortion.

Maria's only friend is B.Z. (Anthony Perkins), a homosexual movie producer. World weary, he tells Maria that he has discovered that the meaning of life is nothing. He invites her to commit suicide with him. She refuses and he swallows a handful of Seconals. Unable to help him, she embraces B.Z. in her lap as he dies.

Maria begins her withdrawal into a catatonic state. She despises her lifestyle: the decadent Hollywood crowd, the empty parties, the nights of drinking and pill-popping. Maria visits her autistic child in a sanitarium but is unable to communicate with her daughter. She drives aimlessly on the Los Angeles freeways, shooting at signs. Divorced by her husband and with her career and personal life in ruins, she slips into madness.

The dazzling look of the film can be attributed to the visual consultant, pop artist Roy Lichtenstein. Director Frank Perry was wowed by Tuesday Weld's performance. "She's a complicated lady and a gifted one...She finally does emerge in this picture. She's really so good in this, so super, and as far as behavior is concerned, her comportment, she was just flawless—I mean just a perfect child. She was there every day, on time, and worked like a tremendous professional. All that talk about being a terror—not a trace."

Tuesday Weld's reviews were mixed, ranging from wildly enthusiastic to disappointing. Vincent Canby of *The New York Times* wrote: "The film is beautifully performed by Tuesday Weld as Maria." Joseph Gelmis of *Newsday* noted: "Weld is not only sexy but eloquent in what she doesn't say with words...She reminds me of a less verbal Jane Fonda—more like early Marlon Brando—implying experiences and knowledge that can't be conveyed by speech."

On the negative side, Pauline Kael wrote: "With her Alice in Wonderland forehead and her calm, wide eyes, she's like a great pumpkin-headed doll, and she doesn't express pain—just a beautiful blobby numbness that suggests childlike abstraction as much as suffering." John Simon concurred: "Miss Weld, a critics' darling, moves blandly, talks uninflectedly. and looks as blank as an unsigned check; she reveals, to be sure, a perfect inner emptiness."

Tuesday finally received formal recognition for her work when she won the Best Actress Award at the Venice Film Festival for her performance in *Play It As It Lays*. The award helped to confirm her status as a serious actress, but not all critics were convinced. Thomas Meehand wrote in the *Saturday Review*: "I don't agree with the judges at the Venice Film Festival who last summer named her the best actress of the year for her performance in *Play It As It Lays*. Next year, I suppose, the Nobel Prize for Literature will go to Jacqueline Susann."

esday Weld as the town outcast Selena Cross in *Return to Peyton Place* (1961).

rprised by Terry-Thomas in *Bachelor Flat* (1962).

With Steve McQueen in *The Cincinnati Kid* (1965).

Face to face with Ann-Magret in *The Cincinnati Kid*.

With Anthony Perkins in *Pretty Poison* (1968).

Orson Welles and Tuesday Weld in Central Park in *A Safe Place* (1971).

Philip Proctor, Tuesday Weld, and Jack Nicholson in *A Safe Place*.

With Gregory Peck in *I Walk the Line* (1970).

As Zelda Fitzgerald in *F. Scott Fitzgerald in Hollywood* (1976).

With James Caan in *Thief* (1981).

In one of her most memorable made for
television movies, *Madame X* (1981).

With Al Pacino in *Author! Author!* (1982).

Behind the wheel with Robert De Niro in *Once Upon a Time in America* (1984).

Tuesday's performance in *Play It As It Lays* prompted strong reactions from her fans, none more impassioned than that of Foster Hirsch. On November 26, 1972, he wrote a column in *The New York Times* entitled "This Hurts Me More Than It Hurts You." The format was a letter addressed directly to Tuesday Weld in which he admonished her for her performance in *Play It As It Lays* and the direction her career was heading.

Hirsch wrote: "I'm the original Tuesday Weld fan...In 1956, when I saw you in a dopey teenage flick called *Rock, Rock, Rock*, I knew you were special—a movie natural with an edgy, nervy presence and a pleasantly liquid voice.

"In movie after not-so-hot movie you played variations on your own distinctive Lolita: you were the temptress with the angelic face, the cuddly high school minx, the bobby soxer with a difference...In the sort of role you kept on playing, no other actress could touch you."

After praising Weld on her early work, Hirsch criticized her for her last two performances in *A Safe Place* and *Play It As It Lays*. He suggested that she was accepting roles which did not suit her talents and urged her to rethink her career. Several of Tuesday's supporters wrote letters to the editor defending her recent performances.

Tuesday insisted that she appeared only in films she felt strongly about. "Some people just skim through films, saying: 'I don't really want to do this but I need the money.' Well fuck that. I'd live on the streets first."

Tuesday Weld became romantically involved with Al Pacino. Pacino's newly-achieved stardom had come after a decade of struggle. While trying to make it as an actor, Pacino worked various jobs including a furniture mover and usher in an East Side cinema. He spent a year earning $14 a week as a building superintendent. His first attempt at acting so unnerved him that he didn't act in public again for a year. He even tried to make it as a stand-up comedian.

Pacino's acting career received a boost when the distinguished actor Charles Laughton became his mentor. Encouraged by Laughton, Pacino had successes in Off Broadway productions before moving to Broadway. In 1969, Pacino won a Tony award for his performance as a psychotic in *Does a Tiger Wear a Necktie?* Three years later, his Oscar-nominated performance as Michael Corleone in *The Godfather* made him one of the hottest young actors in Hollywood.

When Tuesday Weld met Al Pacino, he had just broken off a five-year relationship with actress Jill Clayburgh. Pacino guarded his private life to such a degree that columnist Earl Wilson nicknamed him "The Male Greta Garbo." Pacino did admit publicly, "We're very much in love. Tuesday's good for me."

Pacino hinted that he was not the marrying kind. "If I have kids, I'll get married," he said. He admitted that he did not handle fame very well initially, citing problems with alcohol, tranquilizers, and marijuana.

When their romance ended, Al Pacino reflected on their relationship. "I had a thing with Tuesday Weld but it's over now. Let's just say that Tuesday Weld is now my favorite drink. Sometimes I walk into a bar and really throw the bartender by ordering a Tuesday Weld. It's something I invented, a Brandy Alexander poured over an Oreo cookie. Tuesday and I used to laugh a lot about that."

Tuesday had little time to reflect on the breakup. She soon had a new man in her life. His name was Dudley Moore.

Chapter 12

Dudley Moore

𝒯uesday Weld met Dudley Moore while he was performing on Broadway in *Good Evening*. The show, which co-starred long-time collaborator Peter Cook, opened in November, 1973, and was the smash hit of the Broadway season. Moore won a special Tony Award for his contribution to comedy in theater.

Dudley Moore is a man of many talents: comedian, actor, composer, and pianist. He was born in Dagenham, England on April 19, 1935. The son of a railroad electrician, he suffered from a clubfoot as a child. Corrective surgery resulted in his left leg being a half inch shorter than his right.

After attending the Guildhall School of Music, he was awarded a music scholarship to Magdalen College at Oxford University. In 1957, Moore graduated from Oxford with a B.A. in music and the following year earned a second degree in composition. His ambition was to become a choirmaster or an organist.

After graduation, Moore performed as a jazz pianist in England and the United States. In 1960, he was invited to appear in a late-night comic revue called *Beyond the Fringe*. The other members of the company were all Oxford and Cambridge graduates: Jonathan Miller, Peter Cook, and Alan Bennett. The show consisted of routines ranging from scathing political satire to zany slapstick. Moore's contribution to *Beyond the Fringe* was mainly musical although it became apparent that he did have a gift for comedy. *Beyond the Fringe* was an enormous hit, running two years in London followed by another two years on Broadway. When asked to define his own unique brand of humor, Moore replied, "I have a very ribald sense of humor, which is conventionally known as obscene."

Next, Dudley Moore teamed with Peter Cook on a popular BBC television series, *Not Only...But Also*. In 1966, Moore and Cook made their screen debuts in *The Wrong Box* and teamed again the following year in *Bedazzled*, a comic version of the Faust legend. Over the next few years the versatile Moore starred in London in the Woody Allen play, *Play It Again, Sam*; was the dormouse in the film

Alice's Adventures in Wonderland; wrote musical scores for several films; and recorded best-selling jazz albums.

From the beginning, Dudley Moore's relationship with Tuesday Weld was both intensely romantic and stormy. Both Tuesday and Dudley had been divorced (Moore was previously married to the beautiful British actress Suzy Kendall) and neither was inclined to rush into another marriage. When Tuesday became pregnant, the couple decided to marry. They were wed on September 20, 1975, in Las Vegas. Tuesday moved into Moore's mansion in London.

The birth of their son Patrick caused Dudley to rethink his concept of fatherhood. "I was afraid of the idea of a child," he said. "Then it happened, and I must say it's the best thing that's ever happened to me. Once it happened, I loved it. If I had my way, though, I probably wouldn't have had him. But Tuesday wanted to—and there he was."

It took Dudley Moore time to get used to Tuesday's idiosyncrasies. Probably the most irritating to him was her habit of leaving doors open. She would leave open cupboard and closet doors. Tuesday tried to explain the reason for her open door policy: "I like everything open. Everything. I don't like shut doors. I like to see. In the kitchen, I like to see all the spices, all the food...and if I don't see it, it doesn't exist. Maybe it's existential."

What annoyed Dudley Moore the most was Tuesday's strange habit of opening the refrigerator door and standing in front of it. This was particularly embarrassing when it occurred at someone else's house. Tuesday elaborated, "I couldn't tell you that the fridge is a father figure or a mother figure…I wasn't really aware of it until people complained. It was completely unconscious. I would hear, 'Could you please shut that door? We're going to lose all the ice. The food will go bad.'"

Tuesday temporarily put her acting career on hold to devote time to her marriage and motherhood. She did find time to star in a couple of movies. The made-for TV movies were beginning to gain popularity and Tuesday found them to be an effective showcase for her talents.

Her first made-for-television movie was *Reflections of Murder*, which aired on ABC on November 24, 1974. *Reflections of Murder* was a remake of the classic French thriller, *Diabolique*. *Reflections* was directed by John Badham, a veteran television director, who soon made a name in feature films such as *Saturday Night Fever* and *Whose Life Is It Anyway?*

The movie, shot in Washington, also starred Joan Hackett, Sam Waterston, and Michael Lerner. Tuesday played the role Simone Signoret had portrayed in the original version. Michael Elliott (Sam Waterston) is an abusive schoolmaster at a boys school located on Puget Sound. His wife Claire (Joan Hackett), and his mistress Vicky (Tuesday Weld) devise a plan to murder him and make his death appear to be an accident. The plan appears to be foolproof.

However, the two women are shocked when his body mysteriously disappears. For the rest of the movie, Vicky and Claire are terrorized by Michael's "phantom." The stylish film was probably Tuesday's best made-for-television movie.

The success of *Reflections of Murder* prompted her to star in a second made-for-television movie. *F. Scott Fitzgerald in Hollywood* was first aired on ABC on May 16, 1976. The movie was written by Emmy winner James Costigan. Two years earlier, Costigan had written another TV movie about Fitzgerald entitled *F. Scott Fitzgerald and the Last of the Belles*, starring Richard Chamberlain as the brilliant author and Blythe Danner as his flamboyant wife, Zelda.

F. Scott Fitzgerald in Hollywood also boasted a fine cast. Tuesday Weld played the unstable Zelda, and Jason Miller portrayed Scott. The supporting cast featured Julia Foster as columnist Sheilah Graham, Dolores Sutton as Dorothy Parker, and James Woods as Lenny Schoenfeld. The movie was directed by Indian-born Anthony Page.

The movie chronicles the author's life from 1927, the peak of his fame, to 1937 when Fitzgerald was reduced to a hack in Hollywood and Zelda was confined to a sanitarium following numerous mental breakdowns. After the incredible success of novels such as *This Side of Paradise* and *The Great Gatsby*, Fitzgerald was the golden boy of the literary world. He and his beautiful, vivacious wife, Zelda, lived with reckless abandon and personified the Flapper

Age. The twenties ended with the Great Depression, and readers were no longer interested in Fitzgerald's tales of the rich. His book sales plummeted, and his emotionally fragile wife cracked under the strain.

The movie focuses on Fitzgerald's attempt to make a comeback as a Hollywood screenwriter. He visits Zelda, who is confined to a mental institution in North Carolina. Scott, burdened by financial worries, Zelda's mental illness, and his frustrations in Hollywood, has become dispirited and an alcoholic. Although he still loves his wife, he has taken a mistress, aspiring Hollywood columnist Sheilah Graham. There are flashbacks to better times, but most of the action deals with Scott's battles with producers and his delicate, sometimes explosive relationship with his mad wife.

Tuesday's performance as Zelda was remarkable. Effortlessly, she flashed from a radiant Zelda of days gone by to a seductive Zelda to a demented Zelda. Judith Crist, critic of *TV Guide*, wrote: "Tuesday Weld, all too briefly brilliant as Zelda." Film historian David Thomson concurred: "She has scenes as Zelda in the TV movie *F. Scott Fitzgerald in Hollywood* that are as good as any American actress has done on screen."

One television project which Tuesday declined was an attempt to revive the old television series *Dobie Gillis*. In May, 1977, a pilot called "Whatever Happened to Dobie

Gillis" updated the lives of the characters from the original series. Dobie had married Zelda and had a teenage son named George. His beatnik buddy, Maynard G. Krebs, had become a successful entrepreneur and, not surprisingly, Chatsworth Osborne, Jr. was the town banker. While most of the original cast returned, including Dwayne Hickman and Bob Denver, there was no Thalia Menninger because Tuesday Weld was not interested in reprising her most famous role. The series was not picked up by CBS.

Aside from the two made-for-television movies, Tuesday didn't appear in a feature film in five years. When asked by an interviewer what had driven her into seclusion, Tuesday joked, "I think it was a Buick."

She was about to return to the big screen in a big way.

Looking for Mr. Goodbar was based on the controversial best-selling novel by Judith Rossner. Tuesday Weld was selected to play the role of Katharine, beating out a number of actresses, including Cybill Shepherd. The all-star cast featured Diane Keaton, Richard Gere, Richard Kiley, and Tom Berenger. The director was Richard Brooks, a Hollywood veteran with films such as *Cat on a Hot Tin Roof*, *Elmer Gantry*, and *In Cold Blood* to his credit. Tuesday enjoyed working with Brooks, calling him a "fabulous director."

Theresa Dunn (Diane Keaton) is a first grade teacher of deaf students. Theresa lives with her parents. Her older sister, Katharine (Tuesday Weld), has always been the popular one, dating the star quarterback in high school. Katharine is a stewardess and is having affairs with men in both Chicago and New York. She is clearly the favorite of her parents. "They think I sweat perfume," she tells Theresa. She breaks down and confides to Theresa that she's pregnant and she doesn't know who the baby's father is.

Katharine meets a rich man on a plane and gets married. She returns home in a Mercedes, wearing a mink coat. She attends a wild party at Katharine's apartment. Katharine watches a stag film while her guests smoke pot. Theresa goes into a bedroom where she sees Katharine asleep while her husband and another woman make love.

Theresa's father yells at her for staying out all night. He reminds her, "You're not Katharine, you know, not by a long shot." Theresa moves out and gets her own apartment. She continues to live a double life; by day she's a dedicated teacher, by night she picks up men in bars. She meets a young stud named Tony (Richard Gere). She's attracted to him physically but fears his violent temper.

Katharine divorces her husband when she discovers that he's "shacked up with some teenybopper." She swears that she's going to give up alcohol and pills and get involved in group therapy to deal with her problems. Katharine visits Theresa's apartment and catches Tony beating her sister. She jumps on Tony and flails away at him until he flees. When Katharine picks up a towel to wipe the blood off Theresa's mouth, several huge roaches fall on her, causing both women to scream. Katharine comments, "The cockroaches are taking over the world."

On New Year's Eve, Theresa goes out to cruise the singles bars. She promises that it's for the last time. She picks up a muscular young man named Gary (Tom Berenger), unaware that he possesses a violent streak. Gary is sensitive because he's having a homosexual affair, and he becomes agitated when he is unable to consummate his lovemaking with Theresa. When Theresa asks him to leave, he goes into a rage and murders her.

The film, probably due to its graphic violence and unsavory subject matter, received mixed reviews, but Tuesday Weld won critical acclaim for her performance. For the first time Tuesday Weld was nominated for an Academy Award. She was nominated for best supporting actress, along with Leslie Browne (*The Turning Point*), Quinn Cummings (*The Goodbye Girl*), Melinda Dillon (*Close Encounters of the Third Kind), and* Vanessa Redgrave (Julia). It had taken almost twenty years, but Tuesday had finally overcome her sex kitten image and reputation as a rebel to be recognized by the Hollywood establishment.

Oddsmakers in Las Vegas listed Tuesday as the favorite to win the Oscar. It became apparent that it was a two-way race between Tuesday and Vanessa Redgrave. Redgrave belonged to a distinguished British acting family which included her father, Michael, and her sister, Lynn. She had been nominated on three previous occasions. On the negative side, Redgrave was criticized for her unpopular political views, particularly her support of the Palestinian Liberation Organization.

The Fiftieth Academy Awards presentation was held at the Dorothy Chandler Pavilion in Los Angeles on March 29, 1978. It was apparent even before the ceremonies began that this was going to be the most explosive evening in the history of the Academy Awards. Most of the controversy surrounded Vanessa Redgrave. Outside the auditorium, seventy-five members of the Jewish Defense League protested Redgrave's nomination. Equally vocal were two hundred PLO sympathizers who supported her. Redgrave arrived in an ambulance, accompanied by two bodyguards.

There was little time for suspense as the Best Supporting Actress award was the first of the evening. As presenter John Travolta read the names of the nominees, Tuesday Weld nervously awaited the announcement. She looked down and licked her lips, then smiled when Vanessa Redgrave was announced as the winner.

As the Academy had feared, Vanessa Redgrave couldn't resist making a political statement during her acceptance speech. When she referred to "Zionist hoodlums," many in the audience gasped while others booed. She inferred that her victory had "dealt a final blow against that period when Nixon and McCarthy launched a worldwide witchhunt against those who tried to express in their lives and their work the truth that they believed in."

If Vanessa Redgrave was convinced her Oscar confirmed truth and justice in the world, others were less sure. Outside, protesters burned her in effigy and held signs which read "Vanessa is a murderer." Paddy Chayefsky, the noted screenwriter, said, "I would like to suggest to Miss Redgrave that her winning the Academy Award is not a pivotal moment in history." Comedian Alan King was also outraged and remarked, "I am that Zionist hoodlum she was talking about." Jack Nicholson was more laid back in his comments. "Who are these Zionists? I've been skiing."

At the Governor's Ball that followed the awards ceremony, Vanessa Redgrave received an icy reception. For most of the evening she sat alone, protected by her bodyguards. The only bright spot of the evening for Tuesday Weld was that her co-star in *Looking for Mr. Goodbar*, Diane Keaton, won the Oscar for Best Actress, although the recognition was for her performance in *Annie Hall*. Tuesday's evening was better than her fellow nominee, Leslie Browne, who had her fur coat and jewelry stolen when her hotel room was broken into.

Tuesday's reaction to being nominated for an Academy Award? "It was nice, but I didn't win. That wasn't so nice."

Chapter 13

Who'll Stop the Rain

Tuesday Weld's Oscar nomination reestablished her as a bankable star in Hollywood. In 1978, she co-starred with Nick Nolte in *Who'll Stop the Rain*, a film about a disillusioned Vietnam vet who becomes involved in a drug smuggling ring.

Who'll Stop the Rain was based on Robert Stone's novel, *Dog Soldiers*, which won the National Book Award. The film's title was taken from a hit song by Creedence Clearwater Revival. Czech-born director Karel Reisz had made several significant films in Britain in the sixties including *Saturday Night and Sunday Morning*, *Morgan!*, and *The Loves of Isadora*.

John Converse (Michael Moriarty) asks his buddy, Ray Hicks (Nick Nolte), to transport a stash of heroin from Vietnam to the United States. Hicks is embittered by his experiences in the service. "All of my life I've taken shit from inferior people," he declares. "No more." He reluctantly agrees to carry the drugs to California.

Once he arrives in San Francisco, Hicks contacts Converse's wife, Marge (Tuesday Weld), who works in a bookstore and has no knowledge of the drug deal. Two men break into Marge's house, trying to steal the drugs. She and Hicks escape, and he convinces her that the only way for them to stay alive is to hide out until he can unload the heroin.

Hicks discovers that getting rid of the heroin is not as easy as he anticipated. Gradually, Hicks and Marge fall in love, but their relationship is complicated by her heroin addiction. They hide out in the desert, where they are tracked down by the criminals seeking the drugs. Hicks is mortally wounded during the shootout and Marge, now totally hooked on heroin, is reunited with her husband.

The brooding film became a cult favorite but was no blockbuster at the box office. Director Karel Reisz was amazed by Tuesday's spontaneous approach to acting. "She's an astonishing but reluctant actress. She doesn't like to be caught working—I think she thinks it's vulgar. She gets it all ready somewhere inside her and surprises you with a full-blown performance on the first take. When you say, 'Cut," she says, 'That was pretty good, wasn't it? Can I go back to my trailer?' Heaven knows where she dredges it all up from, but it comes out fully formed."

Tuesday attributed her acting skills to her remarkable powers of concentration. "I'm able to consciously block out everyone working behind the camera," she said. She preferred no-nonsense directors and loved working with Karel Reisz. "I prefer a one-word direction," she said. "One word—and I can do it good. Shy. Tense. Sex. Fear."

In 1978, Tuesday starred in another made-for-television movie entitled *A Question of Guilt*. The supporting cast included Ron Leibman, Vivica Lindfors, and Lana Wood. The film was based on the Alice Crimmins case in New York.

Tuesday plays Doris Winters, a woman of easy virtue. By her own admission, she had at least fifty affairs since her separation from her husband. When her two children are murdered, she becomes the primary suspect. Public opinion demands that she be arrested even though the police only have circumstantial evidence.

The trial is more an indictment of her lifestyle than a presentation of evidence. The judge warns the prosecution that he is going to dismiss the case unless incriminating evidence is produced. The prosecutor pressures one of Doris' ex-lovers, Melvin Duvall (Alex Rocco), to testify that she confessed to him that she murdered her children. Although there is doubt about her guilt, the dubious testimony results in a manslaughter conviction.

While Tuesday was busy on her own projects, her husband's film career was taking off. Dudley Moore once again teamed with Peter Cook in *The Hound of the Baskervilles*, a British spoof of the classic Sherlock Holmes story in which he played Dr. Watson. The film represented the end of their long-time collaboration. When he was asked the reasons for the split, Moore joked, "We went just about as far as we could with filth—pure filth."

It was his next film, *Foul Play* (1978), which marked his American breakthrough. Moore played Stanley Tibbets, a sex-obsessed, would-be swinger who tries unsuccessfully to seduce Goldie Hawn in his bachelor pad. The comic highlight of the film was Moore doing a strip tease to disco music amid the inflated dolls and other sexual paraphernalia.

Moore had been in therapy since 1964, and it led indirectly to his big break in Hollywood. He was attending the Los Angeles Therapy Group when he became acquainted with director Blake Edwards. They met once before at a party; Edwards remembered Moore entertaining the guests by demonstrating how various nationalities throw up. At the time, Edwards was developing a new film, *The Ferret*, which was a spinoff of his enormously successful Pink Panther series. When his star, Peter Sellers, died suddenly of a heart attack, Dudley Moore was offered the role of the bumbling secret agent, but the film was never made.

Simultaneously, Edwards was working on *10*, a film about a middle-aged man's obsessive pursuit of a beautiful young woman. The star, George Segal, walked off the set in a dispute, and Edwards replaced him with Dudley Moore. The film made Bo Derek a star and Dudley Moore a superstar. He could now command a seven-figure salary per picture. "Cuddly Dudley" became a sex symbol, a status he enjoyed. "I think my own desire to be loved is what makes me sexually attractive," he said. "My ideal career would be fucking myself into the grave."

As Dudley Moore's film career prospered, his marriage to Tuesday Weld deteriorated. There were periodic separations; Moore insisted there were as many as twenty. He described their stormy relationship: "We were too tempestuous, although tempestuous is too romantic a word to describe our relationship. But we did know how to fight nicely...We were always arguing and fighting. It made life interesting and sort of exhausting."

Moore believed the fights may have had a therapeutic value. "In many ways, I think we challenged each other all the time. In a sense, she's very perceptive about feelings, and if she felt I was trying to disguise something, she would challenge me by being humorous or teasing me. But now I realize that's not a bad thing. We were fighting for a purpose. There was nothing wrong with it."

The fighting ended in 1980, when the couple filed for divorce after five years of marriage. Moore admitted, "I'm difficult and no one can live with me." Tuesday was granted custody of their son, Patrick. Dudley Moore described the divorce as "amicable." Tuesday was less diplomatic in her appraisal of her ex-spouse. "He's a major asshole," she said. When she was asked why the marriage did not last, she replied, "I don't know how marriages work, period."

Ironically, at this turbulent time in her life, Tuesday starred in a movie which spoofed modern marriage. *Serial* was based on Cyra McFadden's novel which satirized the trendy California lifestyle of open marriages, health food, group therapy, and cult religions. The film also starred Martin Mull, Sally Kellerman, Tom Smothers, and Christopher Lee.

Tuesday Weld plays Kate Holroyd, who lives with her husband Harvey (Martin Mull), in Marin County, where he is an executive at Wells Fargo. The couple have a daughter, Joanie (Jennifer McAlister) but share little else in common. Kate informs Harvey that she's concerned where their marriage is heading.

Kate participates in a women's consciousness-raising group with her friend, Martha (Sally Kellerman). They discuss such issues as "negative family dynamics." The straight-laced Harvey moves out, causing Kate to seek help from Leonard (Peter Bonerz), a trendy therapist. Kate becomes involved in a torrid affair with a younger man, a poodle groomer. She breaks off the relationship when she discovers that the man also has a gay lover. Her daughter, Joanie, joins the Church of Oriental Christian Harmony. Harvey and Kate reunite to free their daughter from the commune. Once Joanie is freed. Harvey and Kate reconcile and move to Denver to restart their lives.

Serial was Tuesday Weld's first film comedy since *Lord Love a Duck*, fourteen years earlier. She demonstrated that she still had a fine comedic sense. *Serial*, like *Lord Love a Duck*, is wildly uneven and much of its satiric punch has been lost over the years as the fads have become passe.

Tuesday Weld continued to divide her time between motion pictures and made-for-television movies. *Mother and Daughter—The Loving Wars* was a television movie which aired on ABC on January 25, 1980. The role of Lillie Lloyd McCain was one of Tuesday's most challenging. During the movie she ages more than thirty years, from a teenager to a grandmother.

The movie opens in 1948, when Lillie (Tuesday Weld) is eighteen years old. She becomes pregnant and tries unsuccessfully to get an abortion. Lillie gets married, but her husband abandons her shortly after the birth of their daughter, Irene. Lillie raises her daughter with the help of her supportive mother (Frances Sternhagen).

Lillie maintains a close relationship with her daughter until Irene goes away to college. During an argument, Lillie tells her daughter, "You've ruined my life. If I had my wish, you'd never had been born." Five years later, mother and daughter are reconciled when Irene marries into a wealthy San Francisco family. The two women are drawn closer when Irene experiences difficulty with her first pregnancy.

Tuesday was thirty-six years old when she made *Mother and Daughter—The Loving War*. For years she had been playing characters younger than herself. In *Mother and Daughter*, she showed she could still be believable as a teenager half her age. She also demonstrated that she could be just as convincing as a grandmother.

Tuesday's versatility would again be showcased in her next made-for-television movie, *Madame X*, which aired on NBC on March 16, 1981. It was the seventh film version of the soap opera based on the Alexandre Bisson play. *Madame X* also starred Eleanor Parker, Jeremy Brett, and Len Cariou. The movie was directed by Robert Ellis Miller, best known for his direction of *The Heart Is a Lonely Hunter*.

The television movie was an updated version of the now-familiar story. Weld played Holly Richardson, an airline stewardess who marries a potential presidential candidate. She is forced to abandon her husband and daughter by her mother-in-law (Eleanor Parker) to avoid scandal. When Holly is accused of murder twenty-five years later, she is defended by her daughter, who is unaware she is her mother. Tuesday's performance as the self-sacrificing Madame X brought new life to tired old material.

Tuesday's next feature film project was a crime caper entitled *Thief*. Its director was Michael Mann, who had just won an Emmy for his direction of the made-for-television movie *The Jericho Mile*. *Thief* marked his big screen directorial debut. Three years later, Mann created *Miami Vice*, a television series whose slick style was tremendously influential in the 1980s.

Tuesday's costar in *Thief* was James Caan. Before he turned to acting, Caan worked as a bouncer and a carrier of the hindquarters of beef. In 1971, he made a lasting impression as the terminally ill football player, Brian Piccolo, in *Brian's Song*. The next year his stardom was confirmed when he received an Oscar nomination for his performance as the hot-headed Sonny Corleone in *The Godfather*.

In *Thief*, James Caan plays Frank, a big-time jewel thief who has served eleven years in prison. After he is released from prison, Frank works at an automobile dealership in Chicago. Frank hopes to do one more big jewel heist so he will have enough money to retire.

He meets Jessie (Tuesday Weld), a cashier in a restaurant. Frank is instantly attracted to Jessie and determined to marry her. He has assembled a collage photo of everything he wants in life: a beautiful wife, healthy child, new house, and financial security. Jessie is reluctant to get involved with Frank because she had been previously married to a criminal. She informs Frank that she cannot have children. Despite her reservations, she agrees to marry Frank.

Frank is introduced to a crime lord named Leo (Robert Prosky). Leo is planning a multi-million dollar heist in Los Angeles, which he promises will net Frank $830,000. Frank and Jessie are turned down when they try to adopt a child because of his criminal record. Leo arranges for them to adopt a baby illegally and pledges to take care of all their needs. Frank and Jessie move into a beautiful new home. Frank has nearly everything he ever wanted. Once the Los Angeles heist is successful, he can retire to enjoy his new life. However, no sooner does he achieve his goals, then things begin to unravel.

Frank and his partner, Barry (James Belushi), succeed at the spectacular jewelry robbery. When they return to collect their share from Leo, he betrays them. Leo kills Barry and tells Frank he'll work for him on his terms as long as he needs him. Frank gives Jessie all his money and tells her to get out, without offering an explanation. He breaks into Leo's estate and kills him in a shootout.

Thief previewed many of the high-tech effects which Michael Mann later showcased in *Miami Vice*. The film was significant for its intricate heist sequences and pulsating Tangerine Dream score. Critic Roger Ebert called *Thief* "one of the most intelligent thrillers I've seen."

Chapter 14

Once Upon a Time in America

$\mathcal{I}$n 1982, Tuesday Weld starred in *Author! Author!*, a film directed by Arthur Hiller, a Hollywood veteran with a number of box office hits to his credit including *Love Story* and *Silver Streak*. After not appearing in a motion picture between 1972 and 1977, *Author! Author!* was Tuesday's fifth film in five years. It provided her the opportunity to work with old flame Al Pacino. Their romance ended a decade earlier, but the prospects of teaming Pacino and Weld, two of Hollywood's most explosive talents, seemed exciting.

Pacino plays Ivan Travalian, a beleaguered Broadway playwright, who is desperately searching for his next hit. At his forty-third birthday party, his wife Gloria (Tuesday

Weld), pushes the cake in his face. Ivan and Gloria have five children, only one of which is jointly theirs. The others are from Gloria's previous marriages. She has the unnerving habit of leaving her husbands unexpectedly. Ivan is devastated when he learns that Gloria is having an affair with an accountant named Larry. Gloria informs Ivan she is leaving him.

If his personal problems aren't enough, Ivan is having trouble writing his latest play. The show's producer, Kreplich (Alan King), is frantic, fearing a flop. Kreplich is reassured when Ivan convinces Alice Detroit (Dyan Cannon) to star in the lead role. Alice is a big Hollywood star, but she is terrified about performing live on stage. During dinner with Ivan, she takes an aspirin before each sip of champagne. When asked why she does it, Alice replies, "Champagne gives me a headache." The play's financial backers, Patrick Dicker (Bob Elliott) and Jackie Dicker (Ray Goulding), are ecstatic when they learn Alice Detroit has joined the cast. Sensing a hit, one of them gloats, "I smell money!"

Ivan and Alice have an affair, and she moves into his apartment. Although he hates to break up the family, Ivan decides to send Gloria's kids back to their fathers' care. Three months after she left him, Gloria unexpectedly returns. She is outraged to discover that Ivan is living with another woman. "You brought a lousy actress into my house," she shouts. Ivan confesses to Gloria that he doesn't love Alice. "I'll take you back in a minute," he tells her, hoping for a reconciliation. Gloria cuts his heart out by informing him she is going to marry Larry on his birthday.

Still hung up on Gloria, he asks Alice to move out of his apartment. Gloria's children, unhappy with living with their real fathers, move back in with Ivan. He decides to bring Gloria back, even if it means kidnapping her. He takes a cab to Glouchester, Massachusetts, where he finds Gloria painting on a dock. She resists Ivan's pleas, and he tries to carry the screaming and kicking Gloria to the awaiting cab. Realizing that reconciliation is hopeless, Ivan advises Gloria, "Don't go near the water. Give the sharks a break."

Ivan returns to New York and finishes writing his play. On opening night, he nervously awaits the reviews. The play is a hit, allowing him to keep his family together.

Arthur Hiller was impressed by Tuesday. "Needless to say, she's a talented and giving actress and a sheer delight to work with. She's responsive to direction...you just touch a button and you get what you're asking...and better! She surprises you with her individualistic way of responding to your requests."

Tuesday Weld's character, the neurotic, man-eating Gloria, was totally unsympathetic, quite the opposite of her next role. She played the spinster, Lizzie Curry, in an adaptation for television of *The Rainmaker*. The program was one of the first productions made especially for cable television. It was aired on HBO in October, 1982.

Geraldine Page originated the role on Broadway in 1954, and Katharine Hepburn starred in the screen version two years later. *The Rainmaker* was taped at the Osmond Entertainment Center in Utah. Tuesday Weld was the only actress in the cast, which featured Tommy Lee Jones and William Katt.

Tuesday plays Lizzie Curry, a spinster who lives with her father and brothers on a drought-stricken farm. The drought is ruining the crops, and the livestock are dying. Lizzie is plain and has never been able to attract a suitor. Her father, H.C. Durry (Lonny Chapman), tells Lizzie it's her own fault. "You hide behind your glasses. You're afraid of being beautiful."

A fast-talking con man, Bill Starbuck (Tommy Lee Jones) arrives in town, claiming to be a rainmaker. Lizzie's father offers him $100 if he can end the drought. Starbuck shows an interest in Lizzie, and she is transformed into an attractive woman, thanks to his attention. Miraculously, a cloudburst saves the family's crops.

Tuesday's next assignment was also for television. *The Winter of Our Discontent* was a Hallmark Hall of Fame production which was first shown on CBS on December 6, 1983. The all-star cast included Donald Sutherland, Teri Garr, and E.G. Marshall. Based on the final novel by Nobel Prize-winning novelist John Steinbeck, *The Winter of Our Discontent* tells the story of Ethan Hawley (Donald Sutherland), a descendent of a prominent New England family which has fallen on hard times. The bitter story shows how a honorable man can be compromised by his pursuit of money.

Her outstanding performance as Margie earned Tuesday Weld her first Emmy nomination. She was nominated in the category of outstanding single performance by a supporting actress. Also nominated were two Oscar winners, Patty Duke Astin and Cloris Leachman, as well as Beverly d'Angelo and Roxana Zal. As with her experience with the Oscars, Tuesday was once again disappointed on awards night when Roxana Zal received the Emmy for her performance in *Something About Amelia*.

Fresh off the Emmy nomination, Tuesday Weld was cast in one of her most complex and demanding roles, the masochistic gangster's moll, in *Once Upon a Time in America*. The film was the last of a series of movie fables directed by Sergio Leone. Leone gained fame in the sixties, creating a genre of films which became known as "spaghetti westerns." The violent films (*A Fistful of Dollars*, *For a Few Dollars More*, and *The Good, the Bad, and the Ugly*) were international hits and made Clint Eastwood a star. The most ambitious film of the genre was *Once Upon a Time in the West*, which cast Henry Fonda against type as a murderous gunfighter.

Once Upon a Time in America was the Italian's homage to the American gangster film. It was his first film in ten years. Leone had spent much of that time preparing for the film which he believed would be his masterpiece. Insisting that everything be perfect, he took six months to select the cast. The ensemble included Robert De Niro, James Woods, Elizabeth McGovern, Treat Williams, Joe Pesci, Danny Aiello, Burt Young, and Jennifer Connelly.

Robert De Niro established his reputation as America's consummate actor. His father, Robert De Niro, Sr., was a leading abstract expressionist painter, and his mother, Virginia Admiral, had been the publisher of a literary journal, the *Experimental Review*, which gave Henry Miller, Lawrence Durrell, Kenneth Patchen, and Anais Nin some of their earliest literary exposure. The ultimate Method actor, De Niro would go to any extreme to insure authenticity in his performance. For his role as a baseball player in *Bang the Drum Slowly*, he spent weeks in Georgia to learn how to properly chew tobacco. De Niro lost forty pounds to assimilate a character in failing health in *Bloody Mama*. On the other extreme, he gained sixty pounds to portray the aging ex-prizefighter, Jake La Motta, in his Oscar-winning performance in *Raging Bull*.

Once Upon a Time in America spans the years from 1921 to 1968. The story unfolds through a complex series of flashbacks covering three time periods: 1921, 1933, and 1968. It chronicles the lives of Noodles Aaronson (Robert De Niro) and Max (James Woods), from their days as youths growing up in the Jewish ghetto on the Lower East Side of New York to their old age.

As a youth, Noodles is obsessed with a beautiful young girl named Deborah (Jennifer Connelly in her film debut). His best friend, Max, is the leader of a gang. When Dominic, the youngest member of their gang, is shot, Noodles avenges his friend's death and is sent off to prison.

Twelve years later, Noodles is released from prison. The gang is offered a job in Detroit by big-time hoodlum Frankie Minaldi (Joe Pesci). One of his associates, Joe (Burt Young), tells them about a diamond shipment he has learned about from an inside source, a nymphomaniac named Carol (Tuesday Weld). During the robbery a masked Noodles rapes Carol.

At a bordello the gang encounters Carol. They put on their masks and ask Carol to identify her assailant. To improve her memory, everyone unzips their pants to expose their penises. Carol inspects each man closely and misidentifies Max as her assailant. She comes on to Max and suggests Noodles join them in a menage a trois. Noodles declines, saying, "I'm afraid if I gave you a good crack in the mouth, you'd probably like it."

Max proposes that the gang rob the federal reserve bank of fifty million dollars. Noodles realizes that a robbery attempt at the heavily guarded bank would be suicide and tells Max he is crazy. Carol, who has become Max's mistress, pleads with Noodles that they must get Max arrested on a petty charge so he can't rob the bank. Noodles informs the police about a bootleg shipment the gang is scheduled to intercept. The strategy backfires when the gang (except for Noodles who wasn't there) is wiped out in a shootout with the police. Max's body is burned beyond recognition.

Thirty-five years later, Noodles returns to New York after spending years in hiding. He has received an invitation from a mysterious government official, Secretary Bailey, who is the subject of a Congressional investigation. At the party, Noodles is escorted to Secretary Bailey's office. He discovers that Secretary Bailey is really Max who admits that he staged his own death. "I took away your whole life. I took your money. I took your girl and left you with nothing but guilt for having killed me."

Knowing that he is about to be exposed as a result of the investigation, Max asks Noodles to kill him. Noodles refuses and leaves the house. Outside, a garbage truck is waiting. Max appears briefly and then vanishes behind the truck. The garbage truck drives away with its blades grinding in the back. Noodles realizes that Max has committed suicide.

Once Upon a Time in America cost more than thirty million dollars, six million over budget. Sergio Leone, the perfectionist, often shot up to fifty takes per scene. The uncut version ran three hours and forty-seven minutes (the European version was four hours and ten minutes). Warner Brothers insisted that an hour-and-a-half be trimmed from the film. Because of the intricate structure of the film, the extensive editing was a disaster. The mutilated version was assailed by critics and ignored by the public.

Critics were more kind to Tuesday. Pauline Kael wrote: "Tuesday Weld is in peak form as a nympho moll who becomes Max's girl....She looks great, and she has a gleam of perversity. She brings the film some snap and humor." Vincent Canby wrote in *The New York Times*; "Only Miss Weld's performance seems to survive the chaos of the editing."

Despite the good reviews she'd received throughout her career, Tuesday downgraded the importance of the critical process. "If everybody becomes a critic when attending a movie, film loses the uniqueness of its art, which is to entertain. It's only a few hours out of one's life; a successful movie demands total involvement."

Tuesday had always chosen her projects by her gut feeling. "I do basically what I feel like doing," she said. "I'm not one to plan ahead." Her follow-up to *Once Upon a Time in America* was *Scorned and Swindled*, a made-for-television movie which aired on CBS on October 9, 1984. The movie reunited Tuesday with Paul Wendkos, who had directed her in *Because They're Young* twenty-four years earlier. Based on a true life story, *Scorned and Swindled* also starred Keith Carradine and Peter Coyote.

Sharon Clark (Tuesday Weld) is a free-spirited divorcee who operates an antique shop. She is swept off her feet by smooth-talking Anthony Ristelli (Peter Coyote). On their honeymoon he talks Sharon into turning over everything to him and then abandons her. She learns that Ristelli is a professional con man who marries women and bilks them out of their money. With the help of John Boslett (Keith Carradine), she tracks Ristelli down after a cross-country search.

Tuesday Weld gave a strong performance as the gritty woman who refused to be scorned and swindled. After almost thirty years in Hollywood, Tuesday expressed a renewed interest in acting. "The truth is I feel the same way toward acting as I did when I started—enthusiastic!"

Chapter 15

Pinchas Zukerman

*T*here was a new man in Tuesday's life: superstar violinist Pinchas Zukerman. Ironically, she met the man who would be her future husband at a concert in which her ex-husband, Dudley Moore, performed as soloist. In 1983, Tuesday Weld and her children attended Moore's debut with a symphony orchestra. He played Beethoven's Triple Concerto at Carnegie Hall accompanied by the St. Paul Orchestra, conducted by Pinchas Zukerman.

Tuesday recalled the evening she met Pinchas Zukerman. "He was conducting and Dudley was playing, and I took the kids to see it. I went with a girlfriend who said,

'Wow, that's Pinchas Zukerman!' I really didn't know who he was." Tuesday met Zukerman after the concert and found him charming and attractive.

Pinchas Zukerman is recognized as one of the world's foremost classical musicians. Born in Tel Aviv, Israel, on July 16, 1948, his parents, Jehuda and Miriam, had endured the horrors of Auschwitz before emigrating in 1947. As a child, he exhibited extraordinary musical talent. His first musical instrument was a clarinet. He was seven years old when his father bought him a half-sized violin.

Zukerman was discovered by violinist Isaac Stern during a trip to Israel in 1962. Stern was amazed by the virtuosity of the teenager. "I have rarely heard as richly promising a talent as Pinchas Zukerman," he marveled. "I fully expect him to take his rightful place among the great artists of our time."

Under Stern's guidance, Zukerman came to the United States, where he enrolled in the Juilliard School of Music in New York. He had difficulty adapting to his new environment. He spoke little English, a handicap in school. His music lessons also went badly. "My music teachers tried to train me like a wild horse," he recalls.

Zukerman was a rebellious youth, and he started skipping school to roam the streets of New York City. Instead of practicing the violin, he played pool. "I was never good at pool though I played day in and day out," he remembered. "I learned a few tricks from the hustlers." One day

Isaac Stern, who had become his legal guardian, pinned him against a wall and warned him that he was in danger of squandering his great talent. The encounter helped straighten out the young violinist.

In 1967, Zukerman shared top honors at the prestigious Leventritt International Competition, which led to a recording contract. Legendary impressario Sol Hurok booked him on a concert tour of the United States and Canada. In May, 1968, Zukerman married flutist Eugenia Rich, a union which produced two children before their divorce.

Displaying equal skill on the violin and viola, Zukerman performed as a soloist with every major symphony orchestra in the United States and Europe. His technique, rich tone, and brilliant interpretations soon elevated him to the ranks of the world's great violinists. In the late seventies, he turned his attention to conducting. In 1980, Zukerman was appointed music director of the St. Paul Chamber Orchestra, the nation's only full-time chamber orchestra.

During his seven-year tenure as director, attendance increased threefold. Zukerman received two Grammy Awards for his classical recordings and in 1983, President Ronald Reagan presented him with the Medal of Arts laurel in recognition of his contributions to music.

Tuesday Weld represented a fantasy come true for Zukerman. He admitted to a friend that he had "always dreamed of driving a convertible with his arm around a blonde shiksa."

On October 18, 1985, two years after they met, Pinchas Zukerman and Tuesday Weld married. Ever since the fire which had destroyed her home, Tuesday had shown little interest in possessions. Her new husband showered her with expensive gifts: jewelry, a sable coat, and a cream-colored Bentley. When she had been living out of a suitcase, her wardrobe had consisted of a few sweatsuits and some clothing she'd worn in movies. "I realize that there was another reason why all those women had fur coats: they really keep you warm," she said. She kept the new luxuries in perspective. "Love is a luxury," Tuesday said.

After being married to another musician, Zukerman seemed relieved to be married to someone outside of the music world. Shortly after the marriage, he said, "At the moment I am a happy man. What I am trying to do most of all is separate my personal life from what I do professionally. Before, they ran too much together."

Because of their separate careers, the couple was frequently apart. Tuesday traveled on his concert tours as much as possible. When she was working, he would sometimes visit her on the set. Pinchas respected his wife's profession. "I don't think I could act," he commented. "It's a highly disciplined profession that requires a tremendous amount of commitment, and it's also a frequently misunderstood business. One needs to be dedicated—the same way I am to the violin."

Despite being a devoted mother, Tuesday was often critical of herself as a parent. She felt guilty whenever she had to leave her children. In spite of her intelligence, she felt that her haphazard education was a liability as a parent. "I didn't go to school myself. I never feel I have enough (education) to teach them or that I can help them with their schoolwork. My history is in personal experience; it's not academic."

At first glance, her daughter, Natasha, seemed to be nothing like her mother. "She's a Mormon, by comparison," Tuesday joked. Despite appearances, Tuesday concluded that her daughter was like her because of her decision to be different. It was exactly the way the nonconformist Tuesday would have behaved.

In late 1986, Tuesday Weld starred in two made-for-television movies. The first, *Circle of Violence*, was aired on CBS on October 12, 1986. The movie dealt with the growing problem of domestic violence. *Circle of Violence* was directed by Englishman David Greene, who had been the co-director on two of the most successful miniseries in television history, *Roots* and *Rich Man, Poor Man*. The cast included Geraldine Fitzgerald, River Phoenix, and Peter Bonerz.

Fitzgerald plays an aging woman who moves in with her daughter (Tuesday Weld). Tuesday's husband (Peter Bonerz) has just left her for another woman. Nearly broke and forced to raise two children on her own, she becomes abusive. She beats her elderly mother, whom she feels had

mistreated her as a child. Tuesday was thoroughly believable as the woman pushed over the edge.

Something in Common, aired less than a month later, was
much lighter material, a romantic comedy about a woman
over forty who has an affair with a man young enough to
be her son. Lynn Hollander (Ellen Burstyn) is a book editor for a major New York publisher. Widowed, she lives
with her twenty-two-year-old son, Nick (Patrick Cassidy). The publisher sends her to the West Coast to work
with a best-selling psychologist, Theo Fontana (Don Murray), who is known as "Dr. Erotica" and is writing a book
on fondling.

While his mother is away, Nick meets an older
woman, Shelly Grant (Tuesday Weld), in a cooking class.
Shelly's marriage has just broken up after she caught her
orthodontist husband making love to his young assistant in
the dentist's chair. Nick and Shelly discover that they share
many interests, and they unexpectedly fall in love.

His mother returns and is shocked to learn that her
young son if having an affair with a forty-two-year-old
woman. Lynn's father, Norman (Eli Wallach), comes to
Shelly's defense, remarking that she's "a lovely lady who
looks nineteen." Gradually, Lynn begins to like Shelly, but
she still is opposed to her relationship with Nick. Part of
the reason for her opposition is that she's afraid of losing
her son. Lynn reconsiders, concluding that she is not losing a son but is gaining a sister.

Something in Common is distinguished by the performances of Ellen Burstyn, Tuesday Weld, and Don Murray. Murray had known Tuesday Weld on a casual basis since she had first come to Hollywood and enjoyed finally having the opportunity to work with her. "It's gratifying to see her develop into a fine actress," he said.

Heartbreak Hotel, released in 1988, was Tuesday's first motion picture in four years. For Tuesday, it was a case of art imitating life. Her character in the film, Marie Wolfe, is a devoted Elvis Presley fan who, thanks to her son, gets to meet him in real life.

Heartbreak Hotel takes place in Ohio in 1972. Marie Wolfe (Tuesday Weld) is a widow who operates the Flaming Star Motel. Other than her children, her obsession with Elvis Presley is her only real interest in life. Her boyfriend, Steve, is a brute who occasionally beats her. "Every day when I wake up I hope things will get better. They never do," Marie sighs.

Her son, Johnny (Charlie Schlatter), concocts a wild plan to raise her spirits. Johnny plans to kidnap Elvis Presley (David Keith) following a concert in Cleveland. He enlists the aid of Rosie, the pizza lady, who bears a striking resemblance to Elvis' late mother, Gladys. Incredibly, the plan works and Johnny drives the drugged Elvis back to his mother's motel.

Elvis, weary of his life on the road, agrees to meet Johnny's mother. Marie is astonished to discover Elvis

Presley in her home. Her spirit is restored after she has a dream date with Elvis. Elvis enjoys returning to the type of life he led before he became a prisoner of celebrity. He advises Johnny on his love life and even beats up Steve. When it's time for Elvis to return to his concert schedule, he kisses Marie goodbye. "I found something I thought I'd lost," he tells her.

Once you get past the preposterous premise, *Heartbreak Hotel* is great fun to watch. David Keith gave a spirited performance as the King of Rock and Roll. Charlie Schlatter was expert as Marie's quick-witted son (he later played a similar role as the title character in the television series, *Ferris Bueller*). As usual, Tuesday Weld gave an effective performance. Lynn Darling of *Newsday* wrote: "Tuesday Weld is just fine as a woman on the verge of surrendering her last hope that things are bound to get better."

Much of the credit for the film's success belonged to its young director, Chris Columbus. His only previous film was *Adventures in Babysitting*. Columbus' attention to detail was accurate right down to the pink Cadillac. Columbus later directed the mega-hit, *Home Alone*.

Tuesday preferred solitude on the set. She elaborated: "When I'm working I never need an entourage or anyone with me. Time has no meaning. I don't notice how many weeks or days go by. I'm so totally absorbed that I really like to be alone. Actually, it's not only when I'm working; I like to be alone in general. I have a hunger for it. I eat up silence."

Over the years Tuesday had the privilege of co-starring with many of Hollywood's leading men including Paul Newman, Elvis Presley, Steve McQueen, Gregory Peck, Jack Nicholson, Nick Nolte, Al Pacino, and Robert De Niro. When asked if there were any leading men she would like to work with, she replied, "Marlon Brando and Robert Redford."

Tuesday's most famous role continued to be Thalia Menninger. The Nickelodeon network, which carried re-runs of the *Dobie Gillis* series, featured a "Tuesday Tuesday" in which only Tuesday Weld episodes were aired. In 1988, many of the show's regulars returned in a made-for-tele-vision movie entitled *Bring Me the Head of Dobie Gillis*.

All the living original cast members agreed to return. Only Tuesday Weld remained noncommittal. Early in the production, she seemed enthusiastic about working again with director Rod Amateau. When Amateau was dis-missed, Tuesday cooled on the idea.

Executives at CBS, realizing that the program ratings would be increased by Thalia's return, made an attractive offer. Tuesday suddenly became unavailable and CBS was forced to look for a replacement. Many actresses were considered for the role, including Kathleen Turner, Teri Garr, Sally Kellerman, Morgan Fairchild, Donna Mills, and Lindsay Wagner. They eventually settled on Connie Stevens.

In a rather bizarre reunion, Thalia returns to town as a rich widow determined to break up the marriage of

Dobie and Zelda. When he resists her advances, the vengeful Thalia offers "oodles and oodles" of money to anyone who will bring her the head of Dobie Gillis. Connie Stevens did a credible job in the role, but for most Thalia Menninger fans, only Tuesday Weld would do.

In February, 1989, *American Film* magazine featured a retrospective on Tuesday Weld's career entitled "The Face That Should Have Launched A Thousand Scripts." While some critics lamented what might have been, others focused on what she had accomplished. Critic David Thomson wrote: "No one was ever more promising for as long. She is, I think, still without peer in America, for her disconcerting balance of intelligence, sensuality, watchfulness, and danger...If she had been Susan Weld she might now be known as one of our great actresses."

After an absence of five years, Tuesday Weld returned to the big screen in *Falling Down*, a controversial film dealing with urban violence. Filmed during and after the Los Angeles riots which followed the Rodney King verdict, *Falling Down* depicts Los Angeles as an urban hell. The story was inspired by a newspaper account of a truck driver who, out of frustration, began ramming cars on the freeway.

Heading the cast were a pair of Oscar winners, Michael Douglas and Robert Duvall. Douglas had won a Best Actor award in 1987 as the unscrupulous corporate raider, Gordon Gekko, in Oliver Stone's *Wall Street*.

Duvall, one of the most respected actors in Hollywood, won an Oscar in 1983 for his performance in *Tender Mercies*.

Joel Schumacher had directed such films as *Flatliners*, *St. Elmo's Fire*, and *Cousins*. "I like stories about imperfect people in an imperfect world," Schumacher said. "*Falling Down* is a movie about the vanishing white middle class guy in a world which has changed." Producer Arnold Kopelson (*Platoon*) had shopped the movie around to various studios without success. He was just about to sell it to HBO when Warner Brothers reconsidered.

Bill Foster (Michael Douglas) is stopped in a traffic jam on the Pasadena Freeway. Fired from his job and divorced, Foster is a man ready to snap. Trapped in the gridlock, Foster grabs his briefcase and abandons his car in the middle of the road. He walks into a Korean market, where he tries to get change to make a phone call. The grocer refuses to make change without a purchase. In frustration Foster attacks the store displays with a baseball bat.

Foster then enters a run-down section in East Los Angeles where he is confronted by two gang members. When they demand his briefcase, he beats them with the baseball bat. Later, they attempt to kill him in a drive-by shooting. Miraculously, Foster is unhurt, although several innocent bystanders are wounded. The speeding car of the gang members goes out of control and crashes, killing all but one of the occupants. Foster removed a gym bag of weapons from the vehicle.

The police are aware of the crime spree but have not yet determined who is responsible. Detective Prendergast (Robert Duvall) is working his last day on the force. His wife (Tuesday Weld) is constantly phoning the station, pleading with him to come home. She wants the couple to retire to Arizona, far away from the Los Angeles urban crime scene.

Meanwhile, Foster stops at a military surplus store run by a white supremacist (Frederic Forrest), who realizes Foster is the man the police are looking for. He tells him that he admires what he is doing and offers to supply weapons. Disgusted, Foster refuses to be associated with him. The surplus store owner threatens to turn him in and is killed by Foster.

Foster continues his journey across the city. He repeatedly phones his ex-wife (Barbara Hershey), asking permission to see his daughter who is having a birthday party. She refuses and calls the police for protection. Prendergast confronts Foster on the Venice Pier, near his ex-wife's house. He tries to talk him into surrendering, but Foster is past the point of no return. Foster pulls a gun (actually a water pistol) and is shot to death by Prendergast.

Tuesday Weld faced a special challenge in her role as Mrs. Prendergast. The character, once beautiful, has not handled middle age very well. Traumatized by her child's death and the constant danger of her husband's job, she has become a nervous, shrewish wife who henpecks her husband. All of her scenes in the film are on the telephone, yet she is able to convey the desperation of her character through subtle expressions and mannerisms.

Tuesday Weld often said, "I've never been in a successful film—I mean a hit. It's always been a cult or underground film." *Falling Down*, her twenty-sixth film, opened at number one at the box office and earned over 100 million dollars.

Tuesday continued to be selective in her choice of roles. As always, the commercial potential of the film did not influence her selection. She would appear in a film only if she felt the role was right for her. In between films, she taught acting, passing on her craft to a new generation of actors.

By the time she turned fifty, Tuesday Weld had become a cultural icon. Matthew Sweet used her photo on the cover of his 1993 album, *Girlfriend*. The photo shows a young Tuesday peeking through a fur collar. There she is, frozen in time, the perpetually pretty teenager. Coy, yet mysterious, she is the girlfriend any young man would be happy to have.

Henry Jaglom, a friend for more than thirty years, attributed her appeal to her individuality. "There's no one like her. She's unique. She's the freest being I've ever known."

Tuesday looked back on her life with no regrets. "There's always a reason for what I did, if I really did it. It might be a lurid reason, but you can be sure there's a reason.

When asked what she saw in her future, Tuesday replied, "Well, I think the future is a dangerous area in which to even dabble or to touch in any way." She added, "I see the present that way, too."

ROCK, ROCK, ROCK (Directors Corporation of America, 1956). With Tuesday Weld, Teddy Randazzo, Fran Manfred, Jacqueline Kerr, Alan Freed, Frankie Lymon and the Teenagers, The Moonglows, Chuck Berry, The Flamingos, Johnny Burnette Trio, LaVern Baker. Director, Will Price.

RALLY ROUND THE FLAG, BOYS! (Twentieth Century Fox, 1958). With Paul Newman, Joanne Woodward, Joan Collins, Jack Carson, Dwayne Hickman, Tuesday Weld, Gale Gordon. Director, Leo McCarey.

THE FIVE PENNIES (Paramount, 1959). Danny Kaye, Barbara Bel Geddes, Louis Armstrong, Harry Guardino, Bob Crosby, Bobby Troup, Susan Gordon, Tuesday Weld, Ray Anthony. Director, Melville Shavelson.

BECAUSE THEY'RE YOUNG (Columbia, 1960). Dick Clark, Michael Callan, Tuesday Weld, Victoria Shaw, Roberta Shore, Warren Berlinger, Doug McClure, James Darren, Duane Eddy. Director, Paul Wendkos.

HIGH TIME (Twentieth Century Fox, 1960). Bing Crosby, Tuesday Weld, Fabian, Nicole Mauray, Richard Beymer, Yvonne Craig, Jimmy Boyd, Gavin McLeod. Director, Blake Edwards.

SEX KITTENS GO TO COLLEGE (Allied Artists, 1960). Mamie Van Doren, Tuesday Weld, Mijanou Bardot, Mickey Shaughnessy, Louis Nye, Pamela Mason, Martin Milner, Conway Twitty, Jackie Coogan, John Carradine, Vampira, Woo Woo Grabowski. Director, Albert Zugsmith.

THE PRIVATE LIVES OF ADAM AND EVE (Universal, 1961). Mickey Rooney. Mamie Van Doren, Fay Spain, Mel Torme, Martin Milner, Tuesday Weld, Cecil Kellaway, Paul Anka. Directors, Albert Zugsmith, Mickey Rooney.

WILD IN THE COUNTRY (Twentieth Century Fox, 1961). Elvis Presley, Hope Lange, Tuesday Weld, Millie Perkins, Rafer Johnson, John Ireland, Gary Lockwood, Christina Crawford. Director, Philip Dunne.

RETURN TO PEYTON PLACE (Twentieth Century Fox, 1961). Carol Lynley, Jeff Chandler, Eleanor Parker, Mary Astor, Tuesday Weld, Robert Sterling, Luciana Paluzzi, Brett Halsey, Gunnar Hellstrom. Director, Jose Ferrer.

BACHELOR FLAT (Twentieth Century Fox, 1962). Tuesday Weld, Richard Beymer, Terry-Thomas, Celeste Holm. Director, Frank Tashlin.

SOLDIER IN THE RAIN (Allied Artists, 1963). Jackie Gleason, Steve McQueen, Tuesday Weld, Tony Bill, Tom Poston, Ed Nelson, Adam West. Director, Ralph Nelson.

I'LL TAKE SWEDEN (United Artists, 1965). Bob Hope, Dina Merrill, Tuesday Weld, Frankie Avalon, Jeremy Slate. Director, Frederick de Cordova.

THE CINCINNATI KID (M-G-M, 1965). Steve McQueen, Edward G. Robinson, Ann-Margret, Karl Malden, Tuesday Weld, Joan Blondell, Rip Torn, Jack Weston, Cab Calloway. Director, Norman Jewison.

LORD LOVE A DUCK (United Artists, 1966). Roddy McDowall, Tuesday Weld, Lola Albright, Martin West, Ruth Gordon, Harvey Korman. Director, George Axelrod.

PRETTY POISON (Twentieth Century Fox, 1968). Anthony Perkins, Tuesday Weld, Beverly Garland, John Randolph. Director, Noel Black.

I WALK THE LINE (Columbia, 1970). Gregory Peck, Tuesday Weld, Estelle Parsons, Ralph Meeker, Lonny Chapman, Charles Durning. Director, John Frankenheimer.

A SAFE PLACE (Columbia, 1971). Tuesday Weld, Jack Nicholson, Orson Welles, Philip Proctor, Gwen Welles. Director, Henry Jaglom.

PLAY IT AS IT LAYS (Universal, 1972). Tuesday Weld, Anthony Perkins, Tammy Grimes, Adam Roarke. Director, Frank Perry.

REFLECTIONS OF MURDER (ABC, Made for Television Movie, 1974). Tuesday Weld, Joan Hackett, Sam Waterston, Lucille Benson, Michael Lerner. Director, John Badham.

F. SCOTT FITZGERALD IN HOLLYWOOD (ABC, Made for Television Movie, 1976). Jason Miller, Tuesday Weld, Julia Foster, Dolores Sutton, Michael Lerner, John Randolph, James Woods. Director, Anthony Page.

LOOKING FOR MR. GOODBAR (Paramount, 1977). Diane Keaton, Tuesday Weld, William Atherton, Richard Kiley, Richard Gere, Alan Feinstein, Tom Berenger, LeVar Burton. Director, Richard Brooks.

A QUESTION OF GUILT (CBS, Made for Television Movie, 1978). Tuesday Weld, Ron Leibman, Peter Masterson, Alex Rocco, Viveca Lindfors, Lana Wood. Director, Robert Butler.

WHO'LL STOP THE RAIN (United Artists, 1978). Nick Nolte, Tuesday Weld, Michael Moriarty, Anthony Zerbe, Richard Masur, Ray Sharkey. Director, Karel Reisz.

SERIAL (Paramount, 1980). Martin Mull, Tuesday Weld, Sally Kellerman, Christopher Lee, Bill Macy, Peter Bonerz, Tom Smothers. Director, Bill Persky.

MOTHER AND DAUGHTER—THE LOVING WAR (ABC, Made for Television Movie, 1980). Tuesday Weld, Francis Sternhagen, Kathleen Beller, Jeanne Lange, Edward Winter, Harry Chapin. Director, Burt Brinckerhoff.

THIEF (United Artists, 1981). James Caan, Tuesday Weld, Willie Nelson, James Belushi, Robert Prosky. Director, Michael Mann.

MADAME X (NBC, Made for Television Movie, 1981). Tuesday Weld, Granville Van Dusen, Eleanor Parker, Randi Martin, Martina Deignan, Len Cariou, Jeremy Brett, Jeremy Stiller. Director, Robert Ellis Miller.

AUTHOR! AUTHOR! (Twentieth Century Fox, 1982). Al Pacino, Dyan Cannon, Tuesday Weld, Alan King, Bob Dishy, Bob Elliot, Ray Goulding. Director, Arthur Hiller.

THE WINTER OF OUR DISCONTENT (CBS, Made for Television Movie, 1983). Donald Sutherland, Teri Garr, Tuesday Weld, Michael Gazzo, Richard Masur, E.G. Marshall. Director, Waris Hussein.

ONCE UPON A TIME IN AMERICA (Warner Brothers, 1984). Robert DeNiro, James Woods, Elizabeth McGovern, Joe Pesci, Burt Young, Tuesday Weld, Treat Williams, Danny Aiello, William Forsythe, Jennifer Connelly. Director, Sergio Leone.

SCORNED AND SWINDLED (CBS, Made for Television Movie, 1984). Tuesday Weld, Keith Carradine, Peter Coyote, Sheree North. Director, Paul Wendkos.

CIRCLE OF VIOLENCE (CBS, Made for Television Movie, 1986). Tuesday Weld, Geraldine Fitzgerald, Peter Bonerz, River Phoenix. Director, David Greene.

SOMETHING IN COMMON (CBS, Made for Television Movie, 1986). Ellen Burstyn, Tuesday Weld, Patrick Cassidy, Don Murray, Eli Wallach. Director, Glenn Jordan.

HEARTBREAK HOTEL (Buena Vista, 1988). David Keith, Tuesday Weld, Charlie Schlatter. Director, Chris Columbus.

FALLING DOWN (Warner Brothers, 1993). Michael Douglas, Robert Duvall, Barbara Hershey, Rachel Ticotin, Tuesday Weld, Frederic Forrest. Director, Joel Schumacher.

B I B L I O G R A P H Y

BOOKS

Bernard, Jami, *First Films*. (Citadel Press, 1993).

Blackwell, Earl, *Celebrity Register*. (Simon & Schuster, 1973).

_____. *Earl Blackwell's Entertainment Celebrity Register*. (Visible Ink Press, 1991).

Blumenthal, John. *Hollywood High*. (Ballantine, 1988).

Bookbinder, Robert. *The Films of Bing Crosby*. (Citadel Press, 1977).

Brode, Douglas. *The Films of Jack Nicholson*. (Citadel Press, 1987).

Crane, Robert David and Fryer, Christopher. *Jack Nicholson Face to Face*. (M. Evans & Co., 1975).

Denver, Bob. *Gilligan, Maynard, & Me*. (Citadel Press, 1993).

Dunne, Philip. *Take Two*. (McGraw Hill, 1980).

Ebert, Roger. *Movie Home Companion*. (Andrews McMeel & Parker, 1985).

Esposito, Joe and Oumano, Elena. *Good Rockin' Tonight*. (Simon & Schuster, 1994).

Faith, William and Green, Marc. *Hollywood On the Couch*. (Morrow, 1993).

Fine, Marshall. *Bloody Sam*. (Donald I Fine, 1991).

Freedland, Michael. *Gregory Peck*. (Morrow, 1980).

Goldman, Albert. *Elvis*. (McGraw-Gill, 1981).

Goodman, Ezra. *The Fifty Year Decline and Fall of Hollywood*. (Simon & Schuster, 1961).

Gottfried, Martin. *The Secret Life of Danny Kaye*. (St. Martin's, 1995).

Griggs, John. *The Films of Gregory Peck*. (Citadel Press, 1984).

Hickman, Dwayne and Hickman, Joan Roberts. *Forever Dobie*. (Birch Lane, 1994).

Higham, Charles. *Celebrity Circus*. (Delacorte, 1979).

Hope, Bob. *The Last Christmas Show*. (Doubleday, 1974).

Howard, James. *The Complete Films of Orson Welles*. (Citadel Press, 1991).

Kael, Pauline. *Going Steady*. (Little Brown, 1970).

_____. *Reeling*. (Warner, 1972).

_____. *State of the Art*. (Dutton, 1985).

LaBlanc, Michael. *Contemporary Musicians*. (Gale Research, 1991).

Lenberg, Jeff. *Dudley Moore*. (Delilah, 1982).

McDowall, Roddy. *Double Exposure*. (Delacorte, 1966).

McKay, Keith. *Robert DeNiro*. (St. Martin's, 1986).

Metz, Rick. *The Great TV Sitcom Book*. (Perigee, 1988).

Oumano, Ellen and Smith, David. *Ann-Margret*. (Delilah, 1981).

Peary, Danny. *Cult Movies*. (Delta, 1981).

_____. *Cult Movie Stars*. (Fireside, 1991).

Reed, Rex. *Big Screen, Little Screen*. (Macmillan, 1971).

_____. *People Are Crazy Here*. (Delacorte, 1974).

Robertson, Ed. *The Fugitive Recaptured*. (Pomegranate, 1993).

Robison, Gerda. *Film Fame*. (Fame Publishing Co, 1966).

St. Charnez, Casey. *The Films of Steve McQueen*. (Citadel Press,).

Sanford, Herb. *Ladies and Gentlemen: The Garry Moore Show*. (Stein & Day, 1976).

Sarris, Andrew. *Confessions of a Cultist*. (Simon & Schuster, 1970).

Shepard, Sam. *Motel Chronicles*. (City Lights, 1982).

Shepherd, Donald. *Jack Nicholson*. (St. Martin's, 1991).

Simon, John. *Movies Into Film*. (Delta, 1971).

Sinclair, Marianne. *Hollywood Lolitas*. (Henry Holt, 1988).

Spada, James. *Shirley & Warren*. (Collier, 1985).

Stanley, Billy. *Elvis, My Brother*. (St. Martin's, 1989).

Thomas-Terry and Daum, Terry. *Terry-Thomas Tells Tales*. (Robson, 1990).

Thompson, Charles. *Bing*. (David McKay, 1975).

Thomson, David. *A Biographical Dictionary of Film*. (Knopf, 1994).

Vale, V. and Juno, Andrea. *Incredibly Strange Music*. (Re/Search Books, 1993).

Van Doren, Mamie. *Playing the Field*. Putnam, 1987).

Vallenga, Dick. *Elvis and the Colonel*. (Delacorte, 1988).

Weldon, Michael. *The Psychotronic Encyclopedia of Film*. (Ballantine, 1983).

Wiley, Mason and Bona, Damien. *Inside Oscar*. (Ballantine, 1993).

Worth, Fred and Tamerius, Steve. *Elvis: His Life from A to Z.* (Contemporary, 1988).

Yule, Andrew. *Life on the Wire.* (Donald I Fine, 1981).

PERIODICALS

Archer, Eugene. "Give Him Tuesday—Sunday, Monday, Always." *New York Times*, December 13, 1970.

Ardmore, Jane. "My Nights Are All Tuesday." *Photoplay*, January, 1962.

Barra, Allen. "Tuesday Weld." *American Film*, January, 1989.

Borie, Marcia. "Almost All My Life I've Been An Outsider." *Photoplay*, June, 1960.

Borie, Marcia. "My Tuesday Is Tuesday." *Photoplay*, March, 1959.

_____. "Circle of Violence." *Variety*, October 15, 1986.

Clayton, Dick. "How I Discovered Tuesday Weld." *Movie Mirror*, July, 1966.

Dayton, Mark. "Teenage Sophisticate." *Screenland*, July, 1959.

_____. "I Lead My Own Life." *Screenland*, May, 1960.

Dean, Robert. "Can Tuesday Hold on to Elvis?" *Photoplay*, September, 1960.

Deer, Robert. "Beatnik with Brains." *TV Radio Mirror*, November, 1958.

Dinter, Charlotte. "If They're In Love, Why Aren't They Thinking of Marriage?" *Photoplay*, September, 1962.

Douglas, Adam. "Tuesday Weld—The Child Who Acts Like a Woman." *Cosmopolitan*, November, 1960.

_____. "Dudley Moore Scores a Perfect 10." *Rolling Stone*, November 29, 1979.

Flatley, Guy. "Most of All, Tuesday Remembers Mama." *New York Times*, November 7, 1971.

_____. "The Girl Called Tuesday." *Newsweek*, October 5, 1959.

_____. "Have Heart—Will Love." *Photoplay*, September 1961.

Hickman, Dwayne. "I Dig Pencils, I Dig Books Cause That's the Way I Win Tuesday's Loving Looks." *Photoplay*, November, 1959.

Hirsch, Foster. "This Hurts Me More Than It Hurts You." *New York Times*, November 26, 1972.

_____. "I've Finally Met My Master." *Photoplay*, October, 1961.

Johnson, Milt. "Living in Another Woman's Shadow." *Photoplay*, August, 1961.

Lester, Peter. "DM Staggers to Fame in Arthur But His Biggest Smash Is Six Foot Susan Anton." *People*, September 14, 1981.

Lewis, Richard Warren. "Hollywood's New Breed of Soft Young Men." *Saturday Evening Post*, December 1, 1962.

_____. "Tuesday Past, Tuesday Present." *Saturday Evening Post*, April 11, 1964.

Marshall, Ruth. "Why Every Day Is Monday for Tuesday." *TV Headliner*, March, 1960.

Miller, Edwin. "Talent Busting at the Seams." *Seventeen*, October, 1961.

_____. "Who Is Tuesday Weld?" *Seventeen*, May, 1961.

_____. "No, Sir Cedric, She Is Not a Weekday Machine Tool." *TV Guide*, July 9, 1962.

Ronan, Margaret. "If It's Monday, It Must Be Tuesday." *Senior Scholastic*, December 13, 1971.

Saroyan, Lucy. "Stormy Tuesday." *Interview*, October, 1988.

Shearer, Lloyd. "Tuesday Weld, Is She Marilyn Monroe's Successor?" *Parade*, October 14, 1962.

_____. "Something In Common." *Variety*, November 12, 1986.

_____. "Suddenly It's Tuesday." *Coronet*, September, 1959.

_____. "The Survival of Tuesday." *Time*, May 15, 1972.

Thomson, David. "Tuesday's Sisters." *Film Comment*, March-April, 1985.

_____. "The Transformation of Tuesday." *Life*, July 26, 1963.

_____. "Tuesday Weld." *Interview*, March, 1993.

_____. "Tuesday Weld at 15: She's Past the Awkward Age." *Look*, May 26, 1959.

_____. "Tuesday Weld, Girl Philosopher." *TV Guide*, July 30, 1960.

Tusher, William. "Please Stop Those Whispers About Me." *Photoplay*, March, 1960.

_____. "Tuesday Weld Whispered, 'Dick, You're the First Boy Who's Ever Made Me Feel I Belong." *Photoplay*, August, 1960.

INDEX